Cambridge Elements ≡

Elements in International Relations
edited by
Jon C. W. Pevehouse
University of Wisconsin–Madison
Tanja A. Börzel
Freie Universität Berlin
Edward D. Mansfield
University of Pennsylvania

REGIONALIZED GOVERNANCE IN THE GLOBAL SOUTH

Brooke Coe
Oklahoma State University
Kathryn Nash
The University of Edinburgh

CAMBRIDGE
UNIVERSITY PRESS

CAMBRIDGE
UNIVERSITY PRESS

Shaftesbury Road, Cambridge CB2 8EA, United Kingdom

One Liberty Plaza, 20th Floor, New York, NY 10006, USA

477 Williamstown Road, Port Melbourne, VIC 3207, Australia

314–321, 3rd Floor, Plot 3, Splendor Forum, Jasola District Centre,
New Delhi – 110025, India

103 Penang Road, #05–06/07, Visioncrest Commercial, Singapore 238467

Cambridge University Press is part of Cambridge University Press & Assessment,
a department of the University of Cambridge.

We share the University's mission to contribute to society through the pursuit of
education, learning and research at the highest international levels of excellence.

www.cambridge.org
Information on this title: www.cambridge.org/9781009376624

DOI: 10.1017/9781009376587

First published 2023

A catalogue record for this publication is available from the British Library.

ISBN 978-1-009-37662-4 Paperback
ISSN 2515-706X (online)
ISSN 2515-7302 (print)

Regionalized Governance in the Global South

Elements in International Relations

DOI: 10.1017/9781009376587
First published online: April 2023

Brooke Coe
Oklahoma State University

Kathryn Nash
The University of Edinburgh

Author for correspondence: Kathryn Nash, Kathryn.Nash@ed.ac.uk

Abstract: This Element addresses questions of division of labor and concentration of authority among intergovernmental organizations by examining multilevel governance in the Global South. It focuses on the policy domains of peace and security and human rights in Africa and Latin America and the Caribbean (LAC), and its central finding is that the extent of governance regionalization varies across regions and issue areas. In the domain of peace and security, governance is most regionalized in Africa. In the domain of human rights protection, governance is most regionalized in the LAC region. Given the phenomenon of regional specialization, the Element makes the case for the greater explanatory power of regional drivers of regional institutional development. This Element is also available as Open Access on Cambridge Core.

Keywords: regional organizations, governance, global South, Africa, Latin America

ISBNs: 9781009376624 (PB), 9781009376587 (OC)
ISSNs: 2515-706X (online), 2515-7302 (print)

Contents

Further online supplementary material for Appendix
can be accessed at Cambridge.org/Coe/Nash

1 Introduction

Global governance is becoming increasingly complex with the proliferation of intergovernmental organizations (IGOs) engaged across many levels of the global system on numerous issues. We have seen not only a growing number of institutions but also the deepening of institutional capacities and functions (Lundgren 2016, 199–200). Given this trend, there is now significant institutional overlap between global and regional IGOs in terms of membership and mandate. Overlap raises questions about *who governs* – that is, how is labor divided between levels of governance and where is authority concentrated? Another way to ask the question is: "How regionalized (or globalized) is governance?" This Element addresses this question comparatively by examining multilevel governance in the Global South, with a focus on the policy domains of peace and security and human rights.

Our central finding is that the extent of governance regionalization varies across regions and issue areas. We can observe regional specialties: in the domain of peace and security, governance is most regionalized in Africa. Regional organizations (ROs) perform a greater share of peace process engagement tasks in Africa than in Latin America and the Caribbean (LAC), and African RO security mandates and activities pose the greatest regional challenge to the principle of United Nations (UN) primacy. In the domain of human rights protection, governance is most regionalized in the LAC region. The Inter-American human rights system (IAHRS) is more active and influential in the Americas than is the UN system, while this is less true of the regional human rights system in Africa. Given the phenomenon of regional specialization, we make the case for the greater explanatory power of regional (rather than extra-regional) drivers of regional institutional development.

This Element intersects several different literatures, including regime complexity and interorganizational relations (IOR). In what follows, we briefly situate our work in relation to this scholarship, with special attention to the problem of hierarchy within nestedness. We then provide background on the historical development of global and regional IGOs within the post–World War II international order and long-running debates about globalism versus regionalism. This brings us to our conceptualization of governance, which will be employed in the empirical sections. The section concludes with a discussion of the Element's contributions to the study of comparative regionalism.

1.1 Regime Complexity and Interorganizational Relations

The concept of regime complexity has helped scholars to map, understand, and analyze interactions around particular issue areas. Although there is debate on how to define regime complexity, particularly around the issue of hierarchy, a common feature is overlap between and among regimes, which are sets of norms or rules that govern expectations in a particular area (Orsini, Morin, and Young 2013, 29). Alter and Meunier define international regime complexity as "the presence of nested, partially overlapping, and parallel international regimes that are not hierarchically ordered" (Alter and Meunier 2009, 13). Raustiala and Victor identify the defining characteristic of a regime complex to be "multiple, overlapping elemental regimes" (Raustiala and Victor 2004, 299). The definition offered by Orsini, Morin, and Young adds another layer to this – they argue that regime complexes are "a network of three or more international regimes that relate to common subject matter; exhibit overlapping membership; and generate substantive, normative, or operative interactions recognized as potentially problematic whether or not they are managed effectively" (Orsini, Morin, and Young 2013, 29).

Our study speaks to the regime complexity literature, but it does not take a "complex systems" approach.[1] That is, we do not seek to holistically analyze the security and human rights regime complexes in the aggregate. These complexes encompass many elemental regimes and a wide range of national and international-level formal and informal institutions in a dense network of interactions. We seek rather to better understand the global–regional division of IGO power and responsibility in the Global South and thus situate this study primarily within the IOR literature (Brosig 2020, 173). Interorganizational relations allows for a focus on organizations as actors and considers the impact of organizational culture, secretariats, and leadership among other characteristics on operations and interaction (Brosig 2020, 173). Many levels can form a basis of IOR analysis, from the individual level that examines the impact of key decision-makers to the bureaucratic level that focuses on the impact of administrative structures within organizations. This Element will examine the interinstitutional level (Koops 2017, 191). And while IOR research has often focused on organizations in the Global North, mapping relations among organizations within a limited set of issue areas (Brosig 2020, 172–73), we turn our attention to the regional–global IGO nexus in the Global South with our unit of analysis being the region-issue area.

1.1.1 Nested Organizations

The rise of regionalism – and associated shifts in the landscape of global governance – has driven much of the complexity and overlap to which these bodies of research respond. This Element takes regions as its analytical starting point in order to examine how regionalized or globalized governance is within

---

[1] For recent work that does take this approach, see Orsini et al. 2020.

specific regional spheres. Taking regions as a starting point can mean looking at many different interactions, including global–regional, intra-regional, or inter-regional (Aris and Snetkov 2018). One type of arrangement particularly relevant to global–regional relations is institutional "nesting," which Young distinguishes from institutional clustering and overlap. Clustering takes place when different governance systems combine into an institutional package, and overlap simply refers to the existence of a common feature across institutions, which could include membership, mandates, and/or areas of operation (Young 1996, 1–6). In nested arrangements, one organization is to some degree *encompassed* by another (Aris and Snetkov 2018, 8). Some nesting arrangements are more obvious. For example, IGOs that "emanate" from other IGOs (Pevehouse, Nordstrom, and Warnke 2004) may be more obviously nested within the IGO that created them. However, other types of IGO–IGO relationships can be described as nesting. According to Blavoukos and Bourantonis, "'nesting' entails regional or issue-specific international institutions that are themselves part of broader multilateral institutionalized governance framework. Issue specificity and breadth of membership distinguish the encompassed from encompassing organization" (Blavoukos and Bourantonis 2018, 40). If we employ this conceptualization, ROs are very much nested within global institutions, specifically the UN, and this raises questions about how labor is divided and how authority is distributed within these arrangements.

Some existing IOR works take UN centrality and primacy as a given. Blavoukos and Bourantonis emphasize UN dominance in UN–RO relations, arguing that "the UN is the sole agent of collective legitimation in the international arena and the ROs seek the UN endorsement to their actions to convey an image of acting with a degree of moral authority and sanctioned purpose" (Blavoukos and Bourantonis 2017, 312). Our findings challenge assumptions about explicit as well as implicit hierarchies within nestedness. The degree to which the UN dominates a particular governance arena in a particular region is an empirical question, one which we systematically address in this Element. We therefore respond to Brosig's call for more careful analysis of authority in nested institutions: "Nestedness implies a certain degree of authority and directs our attention to vertical interaction in contrast to horizontal. The assumption is that the encompassing institution might have greater leverage over the nested one. However, such a statement reduces influence and power to just one criterion and it is doubtful if a unidirectional effect can be attributed to the concept" (Brosig 2020, 176).

Several studies have analyzed the dynamics of UN–RO overlap in a single region and policy area (Brosig 2015; Gelot 2015), but there is little comparative scholarship on this nexus. One exception is Pratt (2018), who looks across issue areas and investigates inter-IGO deference "in the absence of a clear legal hierarchy" (Pratt 2018, 563). He uses a statistical content analysis of IGO policy documents and finds important variation across policy domains: "Counterterrorism institutions display a clear hierarchical structure, with deference flowing overwhelmingly to the UN," while "Intellectual property has the flattest structure, with deference distributed horizontally among institutions"(Pratt 2018, 575). Pratt's study is especially welcome in light of the inconsistent and often underdeveloped treatment of the question of hierarchy within the regime complexity and IOR literatures. Even when non-hierarchy explicitly features in a conceptualization of regime complexity (Alter and Raustiala 2018, 331), the meaning of nonhierarchy in this context – that is, the absence of a "clear hierarchy" (Alter and Raustiala 2018, 342) or "agreed upon hierarchy" (Raustiala and Victor 2004, 279) – often leaves open questions about the existence of incomplete, informal, or implicit hierarchy within regime complexes. It also leaves open questions about how hierarchy, which we conceptualize as inter-IGO authority, is negotiated and contested. Our study reinforces some of Pratt's findings. We concur that the distribution of authority varies by issue area, and we extend this further, finding that it also varies by region. Furthermore, our methods allow us to take a broader view than Pratt does – we investigate actual governance activity (including task ownership).

1.2 The United Nations, Regional Organizations, and Contested Ordering Principles

Debates between "globalists" and "regionalists" date back to the post–World War II period. At the 1945 San Francisco Conference, the United States promoted globalism and centralized authority in the UN Security Council (UNSC). In response, "delegates from 21 Latin American countries fervently demanded a place for regionalism within the UN Charter" (Acharya 2016b, 112). While only fifty-one states made up the original membership of the UN, major increases in membership took place during the 1960s as many African states became independent and in the early 1990s with the dissolution of the Soviet Union ("Growth in United Nations Membership, 1945–Present" n.d.). The states that joined after the founding did not participate in crafting the UN Charter, as many were still under the yoke of European colonialism. Postcolonial states formed their own ROs during the postwar period, including the Organization of American States (OAS) in 1948, Organization of African Unity (OAU) in 1963, and the Association of Southeast Asian Nations (ASEAN) in 1967. Analysis of global–regional interactions must be informed by the history of the construction of the post-1945 global order (Postel-Vinay 2020, 48). The UN primacy doctrine emerged at a time when many of the countries bound by it today were not engaged in the negotiations. How the UN Charter was negotiated and by whom continues to have ramifications for the exercise of authority in the international system, and states that joined after the founding have needed to navigate the UN system in order to assert ownership and authority within it. These states have contested UN primacy through a number of means, including negotiation or creating their own doctrines.

The UN Charter addresses both issue areas that are the focus of this Element – peace and security and human rights. In the former, it establishes a global–regional hierarchy, but not in the latter. Specifically, it assigns responsibility to the UNSC for the maintenance of international peace and security. The UNSC is responsible for determining if a situation is a threat to international peace and security, and it also has sole authority to authorize enforcement action to maintain international peace and security ("Charter of the United Nations" 1945, chap. VI–VII). Regional bodies are permitted to engage in the peaceful settlement of disputes but cannot undertake any enforcement action without authorization from the UNSC ("Charter of the United Nations" 1945, chap. VIII). In reality, the relationship between the UN and regional bodies is more complicated than the black and white text of the Charter. Human rights appears throughout the Charter, including in the aims and purposes of UN institutions, such as the General Assembly and Economic and Social Council. The global body was also pivotal in defining fundamental human rights through the Universal Declaration of Human Rights (UDHR), which was proclaimed by the UN General Assembly on December 10, 1948 ("Universal Declaration of Human Rights" 1948). The UN Charter does not, however, assign primary responsibility for the international promotion and protection of human rights to the UN.

In both security and human rights, ROs were created by regional states independently of the UN. This is different from the economic development issue area where the UN itself was responsible for the creation of regional agencies like the Economic Commission for Latin America and the Caribbean. Regional bodies have continually renegotiated their relationship with the UN through both their ownership of tasks and the authority they claim. The end of the Cold War ushered in an expansion of IGO authority and ownership both at the global and regional levels. This juncture ended a long period of bipolarity and associated UN paralysis, especially at the UNSC, but also in its other organs. Meanwhile, ROs proliferated and developed expanded legal mandates and repertoires of action in the 1990s. These concomitant trends increased the salience of decades-old questions about global governance versus regional solutions to regional problems, and in the twenty-first century, analysts and policymakers have increasingly engaged normative questions that echo these early debates. Is increased regional ownership in the peace and security domain a welcome anti-imperial assertion of Global South agency, or is this devolution of responsibility neglectful "buck-passing" on the part of the Western-dominated UN system? Should regional human rights governance mechanisms supplant the authority of the International Criminal Court (ICC), or are regional courts unprepared to tackle the problem of high-level impunity?

Subsidiarity is an alternative ordering principle to UN primacy. In international relations, the meaning of subsidiarity is most legalized in the European Union (EU) context (Barber 2005, 313). Its application to the relationship between EU institutions and member states is defined in Article 5(3) of the Treaty on European Union (Maastricht Treaty), which states, "under the principle of subsidiarity, in areas which do not fall within its exclusive competence, the Union shall act only if and in so far as the objectives of the proposed action cannot be sufficiently achieved by the Member States" ("Consolidated Version of the Treaty on European Union" 1993, 6). This text of course did not settle the division of competencies, and application of the principle of subsidiarity has been the subject of subsequent EU treaties and court cases (Craig 2012, 72–74). The question of what tasks should remain with what levels and what is meant by "sufficiently achieved" is the subject of debate not only in Europe but also in other regions and realms of governance that are far less legally, procedurally, and practically defined.

In other regions, the term is most often used in the context of peace and security governance, for example in regards to mediation (Nathan 2017) or peace operations (Baranyi 1995). We also find the language of subsidiarity in research on trade (von Staden 2016), democracy promotion, and transitional justice (Reinold 2019). Scholarly invocations of the term are diverse and sometimes inconsistent. Some discussions of the principle emphasize the authority of lower-level actors. For example, O'Brien (2000) defines subsidiarity as "a principle of power allocation [that] favors delegating power to a lower tier of authority" (O'Brien 2000, 58). Other definitions gesture toward this decision-making power by referring to lower-level organizations as leaders or drivers. Nathan (2017) writes that subsidiarity is the position that "the response to conflicts should be led at the regional rather than the global level" (Nathan 2017, 151), and a joint NGO–IGO report (2016) on Central African subregionalism notes that the principle "is grounded in the idea that sustainable peace is best achieved when conflict resolution mechanisms are driven by those actors who are most affected by and closest to the conflict" ("The Principle of Subsidiarity: The Example of ECCAS in African Crises" 2016, 6). On the other hand, some definitions of subsidiarity emphasize the authority of higher-level actors. According to Brosig, for example, subsidiarity "refers to regional organizations executing tasks assigned by the

UN" (Brosig 2015, 51). Many other uses of the term emphasize lower-level task ownership rather than authority. Knight (1996) describes a subsidiarity model of global governance in which "the more immediate levels (regional, subregional, state and substate) ought to be responsible for carrying out those governance tasks which they can effectively and efficiently handle" (Knight 1996, 47). More recently, Ndiaye (2016) uses language that is very similar to Knight's, stating that "tasks should preferably be handled by the lowest level on which an adequate result can be achieved" (Ndiaye 2016, 53).

For our purposes, we prefer a broad definition of subsidiarity that encompasses both authority and task ownership for lower-level actors: "locating governance at the lowest possible level" (Reinold 2019, 2094). More specifically, we are interested in the degree to which governance is located at the regional rather than global level across Global South regions and issue areas in the post–Cold War era. How much has subsidiarity rather than UN primacy taken hold?

1.3 Conceptualizing Governance: Authority and Task Ownership

Assessments of the actual or potential governance role of ROs often reference two distinct but interrelated dimensions of governance, either explicitly or implicitly. We label these dimensions "authority" and "ownership." Authority encompasses rule-making and decision-making power (often legalized via hard and soft law).[2] Ownership, on the other hand, refers to the degree and kind of governance responsibility fulfilled, or "work" performed.[3] Authority and ownership are conceptually distinct, but their indicators sometimes overlap. For example, human rights bodies that process more cases are doing more governance "labor" (taking ownership), and their decisions are also clearly assertions of authority. Furthermore, as discussed in this Element, we argue that the two dimensions of governance are causally related to one another; greater ownership can lead to greater authority and vice versa. It is still important, though, to distinguish between the two dimensions at the conceptual level, because governance regionalization may involve – at least in theory – a delegation of

---

[2] Authority can be asserted without being accepted (by states and/or other IGOs), and we are interested in both its assertion and acceptance. Indications of if and how authority is accepted will differ depending on the issue area.

[3] In her piece on multilevel governance, Börzel (2021) identifies (1) the production of rules and (2) the provision of common goods and services as key dimensions of governance. Our conception of ownership is related to – but distinct from – the concept of goods and service provision since a governance actor may perform governance labor that does not in fact bear the intended fruit. Furthermore, the outcomes of IGO activities may be normatively positive or negative, and unintended consequences are inevitable. The question of effectiveness lies outside our conceptualization of governance.

responsibility (increasing ownership) without a meaningful redistribution of power (authority).

We therefore evaluate the regionalization of governance along these two dimensions. To assess the relative regionalization of *authority* in the security and human rights domains, we first compare the legal mandates of global and regional organizations. For example, the African Union (AU) has consistently advocated for "African solutions to African problems" despite the UNSC's primacy in maintaining international peace and security (see Section 2). In the human rights domain, the Inter-American Commission on Human Rights has individual petition jurisdiction over a broader set of rights and a greater number of states than does the UN treaty-monitoring system (see Section 3). To assess the relative regionalization of *ownership*, we compare the global–regional division of IGO labor in the most relevant categories of activity. When investigating the peace and security domain, we count peace mission implementation as well as peace process engagement tasks carried out by IGOs, like mediation and commitments to monitor or implement the terms of peace agreements. In the domain of human rights, we count the caseloads of judicial and quasi-judicial bodies, with particular attention to rulings on the merits.

In our case studies, we find evidence of a bidirectional causal relationship between IGO authority and ownership, at least in certain circumstances or under certain conditions. First, we argue that African RO ownership contributes to authority. When these ROs attend, oversee, and make commitments to implement the outputs of peace negotiations, they are carrying out governance tasks, and this is ownership. They are also shaping the terms of the peace and often assuming enforcement roles – this cultivates authority. We illustrate this phenomenon through a case study of Darfur in Section 2. This finding somewhat challenges Gelot's assertion that the Africanization of conflict management has resulted in a situation where "Tasks are shifted [away from the UN], but not power" (Gelot 2015, 150). The shifting of power may not be keeping up with the shifting of tasks, but both shifts are underway. The causal arrow is turned the other way in a second example, where the greater legal authority of the IAHRS may contribute to the higher caseload of that system, relative to the UN human rights system. We address this more briefly in Section 3.

This conceptualization of governance allows us to explore if global–regional hierarchy is unidirectional or if indeed there is the capacity for both encompassing and encompassed organizations to shape the relationship. Are these organizations bound by universalist norms that they did not (always) help negotiate, or are we seeing more nuanced interactions?

1.4 Contribution and Overview of the Element

This Element makes several contributions to the field of comparative regionalism. First, we build on and answer specific calls within the existing literature to decenter analysis away from the integration model championed by the EU, which is a regional norm and not a global standard (Börzel and Risse 2016). As opposed to comparing Global South regions to the EU, we compare Global South regions to each other while interrogating notions of hierarchy within multilevel governance. By examining how regionalized (or globalized) governance is, we take seriously not only the potential for regional ownership but also regional authority. This exploration complements analyses in the broader international relations discipline about the often unacknowledged influence of Global South actors (Acharya 2013; Darkwa 2018; Stuenkel 2016). Our approach also places the creation of the UN and universalism in its historical context that acknowledges its roots in Western dominance (Postel-Vinay 2020, 48).

Second, we approach cross-regional (and cross-IGO) comparison *systematically* by directly comparing IGOs' legal mandates and workloads in order to gauge authority and ownership. In Section 2, we examine IGO engagement in peace processes and deployment of peace missions. We use an original dataset of all peace agreements publicly available through the Peace Agreements Database (PA-X)[4] in LAC and Africa to illuminate patterns of IGO engagement while supplementing this work with existing data on peace missions.[5] In Section 3, we examine commission and court jurisdictions and merits decisions to compare authority and workloads.

Third, we theorize the drivers of regional institutional development and regional specialization in the Global South. Our illumination of the phenomenon of regional "specialties" (peace and security in Africa; human rights in LAC) is suggestive of regional – rather than global or extraregional – drivers.

From here the Element proceeds with two empirical sections focused on the peace and security and human rights issue areas, and we compare regional and global engagement in these domains in Africa and the LAC region. We have focused on these two issues because they feature prominently in the UN Charter. Furthermore, every region of the world addresses them to some degree via regional institutions and treaties that shape their governance in unique ways for specific regional spheres. As such, they are ideal issues to help us understand the extent of regionalized governance. In Section 4, we address the drivers of

---

[4] PA-X (Bell et al. 2017). www.peaceagreements.org.
[5] There are several works that examine peace enforcement, while there are far fewer pieces that examine broader peace and security issues in the context of IOR. One exception is McEvoy 2017.

regional specialization and discuss the implications of the Element's findings for our understanding of global governance.

2 Peace and Security Governance

The broad issue area of peace and security could include a range of approaches from confidence-building measures to coordination against transnational threats to enforcement action in the context of ongoing violence. In order to assess governance regionalization, we examine two major aspects of conflict management: engagement in peace processes and deployment of peace missions. These measures will not show the totality of peace and security governance in a given region, but these are the areas of peace and security governance in which ROs could most directly challenge UNSC primacy. Our analysis focuses on the post–Cold War period onward.

Lundgren (2016) has found that since the end of World War II, the number of peace-brokering IGOs (including ROs) has grown from three to twenty-one. The peace and security mandates and capabilities of these organizations have also deepened (Lundgren 2016, 199). With this growth have come many overlapping mandates, rules, and jurisdictions (Nel 2020, 237), but peace and security is one area where there is some degree of codification of roles, at least on paper. As mentioned in Section 1, Article 24 of the UN Charter confers "primary responsibility for the maintenance of international peace and security" on the UNSC. Furthermore, Chapter VII of the Charter gives the UNSC the authority to decide peace enforcement measures, which can include diplomatic and economic sanctions, blockades, and use of military force ("Charter of the United Nations" 1945). Chapter VIII of the Charter, which is the product of a compromise between "globalist" and "regionalist" camps involved in the drafting of the document (Lind 2015, 32–33), speaks specifically to regional arrangements. Regional bodies are permitted to deal with issues pertaining to the maintenance of peace and security and are encouraged to pursue pacific settlements of disputes in their spheres before referring any matter to the UNSC, but the UN Charter does not grant regional bodies any powers to undertake peace enforcement action ("Charter of the United Nations" 1945). Regional organizations are not powerless though, and as will be discussed, they have pushed for new models for peace and security governance.

This section deals with the peace and security regime complex and focuses on IGOs as the elemental units, specifically subregional, regional, and global organizations.[6] While there are other elemental units in this regime complex,

---

[6] For the purposes of consistency across multiple regions with different models, we refer to IGOs below the continental level as subregional, at the continental level as regional, and organizations the encompass states across several regions as global.

notably states, our primary concern is the extent to which peace and security governance in regionalized or globalized. We are therefore not simply concerned with the mandates and activities of ROs per se, but also with how these mandates and activities compare to those of the UN. We find that ROs perform a greater share of peace process engagement tasks in Africa than in LAC, and that African RO security mandates and activities pose a greater regional challenge to the principle of UN primacy (central authority). We also argue that African ROs have been able to carve out greater authority for themselves by increasing their share of security governance labor, as these two dimensions of governance overlap and interact in practice.

2.1 Africa: The Authority Dimension of Governance

Despite the UN Charter's endowment of the UNSC with ultimate power to authorize peace enforcement, African ROs have been carving out competing authority via their legal regimes. Furthermore, most peace and security governance activities do not rise to the level of peace enforcement, leaving questions of authority open. When it comes to ownership, African ROs are highly active in peace process engagement and peace mission deployment.

The OAU did not have a strong conflict resolution mandate during its first three decades, but this began to shift with the 1993 Mechanism for Conflict Prevention, Management and Resolution. The 1990s also saw the Economic Community of West African States (ECOWAS) cultivate a robust conflict resolution mandate for itself, pushed forward by the subregional organization's military interventions in Liberia and Sierra Leone. The ability of African organizations to engage in peace and security issues was further strengthened by the creation of the AU, formally launched in 2002 after a multiyear transition. Its Constitutive Act enshrines principles that protect African state sovereignty, but leaders added principles that assert a right to live in peace and security. Article 4(h) of the Constitutive Act also asserts the right of the Union to intervene in a member state in certain grave circumstances, namely: war crimes, genocide, and crimes against humanity ("Constitutive Act of the African Union" 2001). The Protocol Relating to the Establishment of the Peace and Security Council of the African Union (PSC Protocol) mandates that the authority to authorize an intervention in a member state rests with the AU Assembly of Heads of State and Government. The AU Peace and Security Council (PSC) holds responsibility for implementing any mandate given by the Assembly and can also make recommendations pursuant to the invocation of Article 4(h) ("Protocol Relating to the Establishment of the Peace and Security Council of the African Union" 2003, 6–9). While the PSC Protocol explicitly states that the PSC is guided by the AU Constitutive Act and Charter of the UN, there is no indication of whether the African regional body will or will not seek a mandate from the UNSC prior to invoking Article 4(h). As Gelot points out, Articles 16 and 17 of the PSC Protocol contain contradictory language about whether the UN or AU has primary responsibility for peace and security in Africa (Gelot 2015, 143).

The AU recognizes eight Regional Economic Communities (RECs), and these form the building blocks of the African Peace and Security Architecture (APSA).[7] There is overlapping membership not only between the AU and RECs but also among many RECs. In Africa, this creates a unique situation where subsidiarity is not only negotiated between the AU and the UN but also between the AU and RECs and among RECs. Within Africa, the primacy of the AU or the appropriate REC is a matter of ongoing debate. A 2008 memorandum of understanding between the AU and RECs regarding regional contributions to the African Standby Force commits these IGOs to "adherence to the principles of subsidiarity, complementarity and comparative advantage in order to optimize the partnership" ("Memorandum of Understanding on Cooperation in the Area of Peace and Security between the African Union, the Regional Economic Communities and the Coordinating Mechanisms of the Regional Standby Brigades of Eastern and Northern Africa" 2008). However, these terms are not defined or discussed in-depth. More recently, decisions from a July 2019 AU–RECs coordinating meeting mandated the AU Commission to "operationalize the framework on an effective division of labor . . . including through detailed plans of action" ("Decisions of First Mid-Year Coordination Meeting between the African Union, the Regional Economic Communities and the Regional Mechanisms" 2019).

The AU PSC sits at the center of APSA. Other components include the African Standby Force and Panel of the Wise among others. Many of the RECs have similar peace and security structures to the AU and seek to promote peace and security in their spheres of influence (Desmidt 2019). However, the extent of this engagement across RECs varies widely across the subregions (Coe and Nash 2020). The AU draws on and is challenged by legal frameworks and precedents from these African subregional organizations, particularly ECOWAS as one of the most active and established RECs. In West Africa, ECOWAS often challenges not only AU authority but also UN authority. In the 1999 ECOWAS Protocol, the organization pledges only to inform the UN of military interventions undertaken by the ECOWAS Mechanism for Conflict

---

[7] In addition, there are two regional mechanisms that have liaison offices at the AU, and these include the Eastern Africa Standby Force and the North African Regional Capability.

Prevention, Management, Resolution, Peace-keeping, and Security ("ECOWAS Protocol Relating to the Mechanism for Conflict Prevention, Management, Resolution, Peace-Keeping, and Security" 1999, 27). This change to ECOWAS's legal framework followed multiple interventions in member states to address violent conflict that did not receive prior UN or OAU authorization. The vagueness of Chapter VIII of the UN Charter leaves considerable room for interpretation, and the interventionist legal mandates of the AU and ECOWAS challenge deference to the UNSC, setting them apart from all other ROs around the world. As Tieku puts it, "The power- and burden-sharing roles of the [African Union] go beyond the UN Charter's paternalistic attitude to regional organizations" (Tieku 2016, 159).

In recent years, the AU has increasingly pushed for a reinterpretation of UN primacy and challenged prevailing understandings of global peace and security norms (Lotze 2018, 219). Specifically the AU has sought to "reshape the norm of primary responsibility of the UN Security Council from being driven by a logic of hierarchy to being driven by a logic of shared responsibility and partnership" (Lotze 2018, 220). The position of the African region on the legality of use of force by ROs was elaborated on in the Common African Positions on the Proposed Reform of the United Nations (Ezulwini Consensus) adopted by an Extraordinary Session of the Executive Council of the African Union in March 2005. The regional body endorsed allowing for UNSC approval "after the fact," arguing that some circumstances require urgent action, but the Ezulwini Consensus stresses that the circumstances where use of force is permissible should be limited to self-defense under Article 51 of the UN Charter or grave circumstances under Article 4(h) of the AU Constitutive Act. Echoing the core argument of subsidiarity, the Consensus stresses that ROs are better positioned to understand conflict situations because of their proximity and should be empowered to take action as necessary ("The Common African Position on the Proposed Reform of the United Nations: The Ezulwini Consensus" 2005, 6). By some interpretations, the document aims to "reconcile the primacy of the UN Security Council with the realities on the ground" – which are characterized in part by the inability or unwillingness of the UN to authorize deployment (Brosig 2015, 68). This speaks to the interplay between ownership and authority: the AU responds to inadequate global ownership with assertions of regional authority (to fill a gap).

From 2007, the AU PSC and UNSC held annual consultative meetings. Then in 2010, the UN created the United Nations Office to the African Union, and the UNSC and PSC agreed to carry out collaborative missions in the field. Finally, the UN and AU created a Joint Task Force on Peace and Security to review situations and issues where there is shared interest, in order to enhance UN–AU cooperation (Lotze 2018, 225, 227). However, several situations, notably Côte d'Ivoire in 2010/11 and Libya in 2011, strained the UN–AU relationship due to disagreements over how to address these conflicts. This led the AU to again push for a new interpretation of the UN primacy norm by setting out three principles for the UN–AU relationship:

> First, flexible and innovative application of the principle of subsidiarity, comprising devolution of decision making, a division of labor, and better burden-sharing. Second, mutual respect and adherence to comparative advantage, recognizing that regional organizations have a strong comparative advantage in their own regions and as such are better positioned to serve as first responders. And third, a division of labor underpinned by complementarity that fosters coherence and limits competition. (Lotze 2018, 229–30)

In 2015, the UN Secretary-General released the "Partnering for Peace: Moving Towards Partnership Peacekeeping" report that recognized effective peacekeeping was based on common objectives and cooperation between relevant decision-making bodies. This essentially recognized that the UN–AU relationship had moved beyond hierarchical capacity building to one based on partnership and common strategy (Lotze 2018, 236). In these long-standing and consistent negotiations, the AU has sought to assert authority through a reinterpretation of provisions of the UN Charter regarding both the role of ROs and the responsibilities of the UN in relation to them.

Relatedly, AU reliance on ad hoc and unstable external financial support of its peace missions puts the RO in a subordinate position to some degree, as "purse-string" power constitutes a source of authority. For this and other reasons, the AU has long lobbied for access to "predictable and sustainable financing through UN assessed contributions for AU-led peace operations" ("Securing Predictable and Sustainable Financing for Peace in Africa" 2016, 5). Contentious negotiations between the UNSC and the AU PSC on this matter have not always been productive, but the AU has "made progress on a number of fronts" – including human rights compliance – making an agreement more achievable in the future ("The Price of Peace: Securing UN Financing for AU Peace Operations" 2020, i–ii).

2.2 Africa: The Ownership Dimension of Governance

Norms and legal frameworks tell us about IGO authority, but authority is only one dimension of peace and security governance. To understand task ownership in this domain, we examine which organizations are "showing-up and signing-up" for peace processes and peace missions. In peace processes, we analyze peace agreement texts to determine which organizations facilitated, monitored, and/or implemented peace agreements. For peace missions, we analyze which organizations implemented the mission.

2.2.1 Engagement in Peace Processes

To paint a holistic picture of the ways in which IGOs are present in – and make commitments to – peace processes, we coded the text of all formal peace agreements concluded in Africa and LAC during the 1990–2014 period. The value of international actors in peace processes is well documented. For example, Bell argues that when international actors are parties to peace agreements in civil wars, it can enhance the legalization of an agreement and assist with implementation (Bell 2006). Peace agreements of course represent a moment in time, and there are many instances where implementation does not match the text of the agreement. However, IGO facilitation of negotiations and commitments to implement agreement provisions do indicate ownership in a process. As Wittke argues: "External actors are increasingly involved in these (peace) processes – not necessarily as impartial mediators in a traditional sense, but as proactive "third parties" who frame the negotiation and implementation of peace agreements having come equipped with a set of functionalist authoritative international standards, norms, and rules for peace in post-conflict constitution making" (Wittke 2019, 265).

As such, peace agreements have become a mechanism to establish authority and assert ownership. Inter-governmental organizations can take ownership of peace processes by facilitating them. Peace agreements can also create ownership by assigning peace and security tasks. Furthermore, as peace agreements are negotiated by conflict parties, they can allow the AU or other body to assist with implementation. This creates IGO authority that would circumvent any need for nonconsensual peace enforcement.

As presented in Figures 1–4, our data show that over a twenty-five-year period peace agreements in Africa were consistently more likely to be witnessed by and facilitated by an African RO (i.e. by the AU and/or by one or more RECs) than by the UN during the period. They were also more likely to include language committing an African RO to monitor or implement their provisions (than to include language committing the UN to do the same). Finally, peace agreements were more likely to include language thanking or recognizing an African RO for its efforts or contributions. We also present these data in terms of total peace agreements in Table 1. This UN–RO division of labor sets Africa apart from other regions in the Global South. In Section 2.2.3, we make the case that this regional ownership contributes to regional authority.

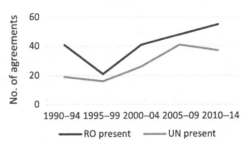

Figure 1 IGO presence at negotiations: Africa

Figure 2 IGO facilitation of negotiations: Africa

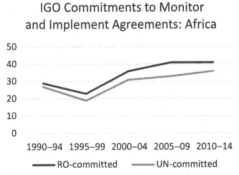

Figure 3 IGO commitments to monitor and implement agreements: Africa

2.2.2 Peace Missions

The post–Cold War period saw the "multilateralization of intervention" (Engberg 2015). At the global level, this entailed an expansion of UN peace missions, numerically and in terms of mandate. These missions became larger and more

Table 1 Agreements engaged by African ROs and United Nations during 1990–2014

	# Agreements: IGO is present at negotiations	# Agreements: IGO facilitated negotiations	# Agreements: IGO commits to monitor and/or implement	# Agreements: IGO thanked in agreement text
African ROs	206	121	169	46
United Nations	139	56	146	36

Note: Some agreements were not engaged by any IGO, and some agreements were engaged by more than one IGO. See Online Appendix for methodology and source material for original dataset.

(Total number of agreements = 435)

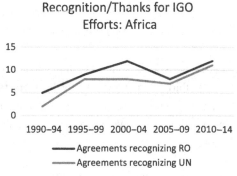

Figure 4 Recognition/Thanks for IGO efforts: Africa

multidimensional over the course of the 1990s, and more robust enforcement mechanisms developed in the twenty-first century, in light of the 2000 Brahimi Report ("Identical Letters Dated 21 August 2000 from the Secretary-General to the President of the General Assembly and the President of the Security Council: Report of the Panel on United Nations Peace Operations" 2000). The UN continues to be the primary body that mandates peace missions. In the period between 1990 and 2016, the UN mandated fifty-eight of the total peace missions in Africa with the AU or other African ROs mandating twenty-eight.[8]

However, the increasingly multidimensional nature of peacekeeping has pushed the UN "to more systematically develop peacekeeping doctrines and

---

[8] Based on data from Military and Non-military Interventions (MILINDA) Dataset (Jetschke 2019). https://lehrstuhlib.uni-goettingen.de/sonstiges/milinda/.

seek external partnerships" (Brosig 2015, 38). At the same time, the increased authority that the AU has claimed through legal frameworks has led to a much more robust peace and security institutional framework enshrined in APSA. The AU and/or the RECs are typically the first responders to crises that require the deployment of a peace mission, relying on a "generous interpretation of Chapter VIII of the UN Charter" (de Coning, Gelot, and Karlsrud 2016, 2). Early AU deployment and subsequent UN takeover is a de facto pattern rather than a de jure policy. It reflects in part the AU's greater willingness to intervene in situations of ongoing conflict to create peace. This pattern was first seen between ECOWAS and the UN in the 1990s, and it has become a "favorite AU model" as AU missions are less expensive and take less time to deploy than UN missions (Tieku 2016, 168). There are also instances of "triangular" relationships among the UN, AU, and RECs in Africa wherein the UNSC maintains political control over a peacekeeping mission through a mandate (authority), the direction and coordination is managed by the AU, and the use of force is determined by the participating REC (Cimiotta 2017, 322). While this pattern may hold in many cases, there is again significant variation across subregions and conflicts.

During the 1990–2016 period, African ROs implemented nearly as many missions as did the UN: thirty-four compared to thirty-six (see Figure 5).[9] Again, this regional shouldering of conflict management burden makes Africa unique among Global South regions. We present data for the LAC region in Figure 6 for comparison.

2.2.3 Interplay between Authority and Ownership in Peace Agreements and Missions

Regional and global efforts to manage the conflict in Darfur, Sudan, provide an example of how authority and ownership intersect and interplay through peace agreements and peace missions. In 2003, the Sudan Liberation Movement and Justice and Equality Movement attacked Sudanese government targets in the region of Darfur, and the Government of Sudan responded swiftly and brutally against not only the rebel groups but also civilians. The government perpetrated war crimes against civilian populations, and by 2004 thousands had been killed and hundreds of thousands displaced (Williams 2011, 33).

The AU involved itself early on by supporting Chad's facilitation of negotiations (Dersso 2013, 231). The first ceasefire agreement was signed in

---

[9] Source: Jetschke 2019. Note: Additionally, thirteen missions were implemented by non-African ROs and fifteen missions were implemented by individual states.

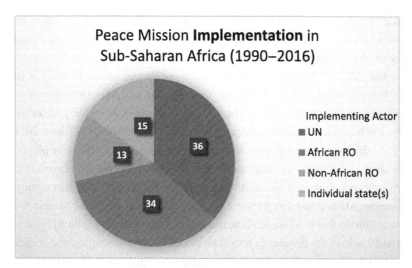

Figure 5 Peace mission implementation in sub-Saharan Africa (1990–2016)
Source: Military and Non-military Interventions (MILINDA) Dataset (Jetschke 2019).

Figure 6 Peace mission implementation in Latin America and the Caribbean
(1990–2016)
Source: Military and Non-military Interventions (MILINDA) Dataset (Jetschke 2019).

September 2003. Negotiations continued over several years involving Chad, the AU, and international actors. Another ceasefire was signed on 8 April 2004, and the agreement stipulated that a ceasefire commission would monitor the ceasefire, while a joint commission would be responsible for responding to any matter brought to it by the ceasefire commission. The AU was named as the chair of both commissions. The agreement also stipulated that the operational arm of the ceasefire commission would be the African Union Monitoring Mission, AMIS ("Agreement with the Sudanese Parties on the Modalities for the Establishment of the Ceasefire Commission and the Deployment of Observers in the Darfur" 2004). The AU deployed about 80 military observers with 300 Nigerian and Rwandan troops to monitor the ceasefire (Williams 2011, 34). At this stage the AU went from supporting mediation efforts to playing a leading role in implementing an agreement. The AU deployed observers as well as troops to protect those observers. While Sudan agreed to this deployment, the AU had to exert pressure on the government of Sudan to gain this concession. In this way, we see how ownership feeds authority. The AU played a pivotal role in the process to negotiate ceasefire agreements, and these same agreements gave it authority to deploy a mission to monitor the ceasefire. This authority was derived from consensual agreement with the conflict actors, including the sovereign state of Sudan. "Showing-up and signing-up" entails both ownership of tasks and the possibility of enhanced authority over those and other peace and security tasks.

The ceasefire agreement fell apart despite the presence of observers, prompting the AU to expand its presence in Darfur. In October 2004, the AU transformed the observer mission into a peacekeeping mission and authorized 3,320 troops. The mission was mandated to "contribute to the general security in Sudan, provide a secure environment for the delivery of humanitarian relief and return of refugees, protect the civilian population in Darfur, monitor compliance of ceasefire agreements, and provide assistance in the confidence-building processes to improve the political settlement processes in Darfur" (African Union Commission 2015, 58). In July 2005, the EU created the EU civilian-military action to support AMIS. Over the course of its mandate, this mission provided equipment, technical support, and training. Although it was created to directly support AMIS and adhered to the principle of African ownership, it still operated on its own mandate and was implemented by an external RO ("Mission Description" n.d.). The AU–UN hybrid mission in Darfur (UNAMID) was subsequently established in July 2007 under a Chapter VII UN mandate, and UNAMID officially took over from AMIS on 31 December 2007. The UN had augmented AMIS prior to the official set up of UNAMID, but the creation of a new hybrid mission meant the peacekeeping mission was authorized by the UN and included an expanded mission and resources ("About UNAMID" n.d.). Since Khartoum opposed a nonhybrid UN mission, and AU partnership was necessary to secure the government's consent, the UNSC "came to see the AU as a broker for a UN presence and consequently endorsed its leadership in the process of implementing the peace agreement" (Spandler 2020b, 194).

In sum, the AU assumed ownership early in the process by supporting Chadian mediation efforts and then codifying its role in the peace process through inclusion in the implementation of peace agreements. The AU was listed as a member of the ceasefire and joint commissions, and it created a military observer mission to support implementation of the agreement. AMIS I was both mandated and implemented by the AU. However, the violence in Darfur continued for years to come, and the AU initiative was unable to bring peace to the region. The EU deployed a mission to support AMIS, and the UN and AU eventually worked together to mandate and implement a hybrid missions with far more capacity. As extraregional organizations increased involvement, they still deferred to the AU even while providing support and eventually taking over the peacekeeping mission. Deference is a recognition of authority to the regional actor. This deference is evidenced, for example, by the EU's creation of a mission to support AMIS and the nature of the UN–AU hybrid mission.

Some have suggested that the regionalization of security governance labor – at least in Africa – has resulted in a buck-passing situation where "Tasks are shifted, but not power" (Gelot 2015, 150), or where the UN is able to "micromanage African peace and security . . . without actually doing the heavy lifting" (Tieku 2016, 165). As the data and case study show, tasks and power are not so easily separated in practice. In fact, RO burden-taking has the potential to advance RO authority, and ROs have been seeking authority through several means. First, there have been direct challenges to UN primacy through the constitutive documents and defense protocols of the AU and ECOWAS, and the AU has also sought to work with the UN to designate a division of labor. This takes the form of the AU taking on immediate response efforts and then bringing in the UN to support longer-term, resource-intensive nation-building efforts. Finally, the AU and other regional bodies have used other mechanisms to establish authority, notably peace agreements. United Nations Article 54 requires ROs to keep the UNSC informed of their peace and security activities, and Article 52(1) implies that the UNSC can censure ROs for acting in ways not in keeping with the Principles and Purposes of the UN Charter. According to Lind, though, in practice, the UNSC does not enforce the former rule, nor does it make use of the latter sanction (censure) (Lind 2015, 35). Instead, the UN has often been an active partner in these efforts as a way to spread the peace and security burden.

The AU has also arguably increasingly been able to shape UN actions, which speaks to its influence. For example, Tieku points to several cases where the AU "co-opted" the UN into a peacekeeping role on the heels of an initial AU intervention, citing these cases as evidence of "power-sharing" between the regional and global organizations (Tieku 2016, 169). Brosig refers to a UN takeover as the "preferred exit option for the AU," due to the RO's resource constraints. The AU's willingness to intervene early – coupled with the UN's superior resources and ability to implement long-term multidimensional missions – creates a UN–AU "dual dependency," despite the asymmetrical dimensions of the relationship (Brosig 2015, 247–49). Observers also take note of the UNSC's rhetorical deference to AU positions on conflict situations on the continent – this speaks to an emerging "gatekeeping" role for the AU PSC (Bellamy and Williams 2011, 826). However, the degree to which (and conditions under which) the UN defers to the AU is in need of greater study.

2.3 Latin America and the Caribbean: The Authority Dimension of Governance

The western hemisphere has developed regional frameworks to address peace and security issues, but its challenges and institutions differ from Africa's.[10] While some intrastate conflicts exist – as well as the potential for conflicts between states – a more pressing concern for the region is domestic instability due to political crises, inequality, and organized crime (Dominguez 2017, 61–62). When it comes to peace process engagement and mission deployment, ROs in LAC have weaker mandates and lower levels of activity (relative to the UN) than their African counterparts.

The hemispheric RO for the Americas is the OAS. Formally created in 1948, this multipurpose organization specializes in the promotion and protection of democracy and human rights, but it also seeks to strengthen peace and security ("Charter of the Organization of American States" 1951). During its first several decades, the organization focused on collective security and dispute settlement. These activities found basis in the Rio Treaty (1947) and OAS Charter (1951)[11]– the "original pillars of the hemispheric security system" (Herz 2011, 29) – reflecting long-running Pan-American norms of legalism, nonintervention, and peaceful settlement of disputes.

US interventionism and co-optation of regional mechanisms contributed to the organization's irrelevance in the 1970s and 1980s. The OAS renewed its relevance in the early 1990s and gained new powers to protect democracy,[12]

---

[10] Latin America and the Caribbean is defined as all Western hemisphere states excluding Canada, Guyana, Suriname, and the United States.

[11] Treaty dates represent entry into force.

[12] Key legal instruments in the OAS defense of democracy regime include the Santiago Declaration (1991), Resolution 1080 (1991), the Protocol of Washington (1997), and the Inter-American Democratic Charter (2001).

especially in response to coups and *autogolpes*. According to Weiffen, such mechanisms can be seen as "means for conflict prevention and conflict resolution" (Weiffen 2012, 370). While we agree that political crisis management is relevant to peace and security governance – and that ROs have been leading the way in this field – the OAS is not unique in this respect. African ROs boast an equally robust legal regime to respond to unconstitutional changes in government. Moreover, the AU has empowered its PSC to respond to these threats to democracy, linking the democracy protection regime directly to APSA.

The OAS emphasizes a multidimensional understanding of security. It adopted the Declaration on Security in the Americas in 2003, affirming that "challenges in the hemispheric context are of diverse nature and multidimensional in scope, and that the traditional concept and approach should be expanded to encompass new and non-traditional threats, which include economic, social, health, and environmental aspects" ("Declaration on Security in the Americas" 2003). Within the structures of the OAS, there is the Secretariat for Multidimensional Security, which has specific offices dealing with drug abuse, terrorism, public security, and transnational organized crime ("Secretariat for Multidimensional Security" n.d.). However, security threats vary across LAC, and "the lack of a shared regional perception of threat inhibits deepening cooperation; and in areas where mechanisms of security governance are already in place, they tend to remain modest, incipient and often rhetorical in character" (Dominguez 2017, 54). Beyond these issues, some LAC states continue to be skeptical of the OAS due to the involvement of the United States and its policies that have interfered in the internal affairs of other OAS member states (Dominguez 2017, 59).

When it comes to direct conflict management powers, the OAS is weaker than the AU. One indicator of this is that R2P is "not part of the vocabulary used within the walls of the OAS" (Herz 2011, 48), setting it apart from IGOs that have increasingly embraced coercive diplomacy and interventionism (Herz 2011, 58). Several ROs in the region have assumed conflict resolution roles – these include the OAS, the Union of South American Nations (UNASUR), the Community of Latin American and Caribbean States, and the Common Market of the South, among others (Herz, Siman, and Telles 2017, 124). However, none of these ROs have legalized intervention in the way that the AU has done with Article 4(h). While many LAC states support the R2P principle generally (Rodriguez 2020), OAS member states have not engaged in a concerted effort to regionalize R2P, and the LAC region presents significantly less of a challenge to UN primacy in peace and security than does Africa.

Also unlike in Africa, there is no framework to manage relationships between the hemispheric organization and subregional bodies. For its part, UNASUR was created in 2008 by all twelve independent South American states, although many members have since withdrawn. The South American Defense Council was also proposed in 2008. It seeks to consolidate peace in South America and make gradual progress on regional security cooperation and defense policy (Weiffen, Wehner, and Nolte 2013, 376–78). Like the OAS, UNASUR endorses a multidimensional security approach, and its organizational objectives including addressing inequality and sustainability as well as specific security issues, such as terrorism, human trafficking, drugs, and transnational crime ("South American Union of Nations Constitutive Treaty" 2011). These overlapping objectives with the OAS do not imply coordination or cooperation though.

2.4 Latin America and the Caribbean: The Ownership Dimension of Governance

2.4.1 Engagement in Peace Processes

According to our peace agreement data, the RO–UN division of labor in peace process engagement is not tilted toward ROs. It is also the case that many fewer agreements were concluded in the Americas than in Africa during this time period. In fact, so few agreements were concluded during 2005–9 (two total) that Figures 7–9 cover only the years 1990–2004. In Table 2, we present data for 1990–2014.

Since our data are based on the text of formal peace agreements and our coding scheme is made up of a limited number of activity categories, these figures do not capture all IGO conflict management activities. For example, the OAS has taken a multidimensional approach to peacebuilding via its Mission to Support the Peace Process in Colombia (2004–present). Not all Mission activities are accounted for in our coding scheme. Among other tasks, Mission personnel have

> "accompanied family members and institutions in processes of the exhumation of mass graves of victims of the armed conflict; accompanied the implementation and monitored the Law of Justice and Peace; monitored during more than 400 visits the conditions of incarceration of members of the AUC, FARC-EP and ELN; and contributed to the design, implementation and monitoring of the Law of Victims and the Restitution of Lands" ("Press Release: The Mission to Support the Peace Process in Colombia (MAPP/OAS)" 2016).

According to Weiffen, Wehner, and Nolte (2013), UNASUR at a certain point had "successfully developed informal ad hoc practices for crisis management", especially in response to democratic breakdowns and interstate border disputes (Weiffen, Wehner, and Nolte 2013, 377). Again, our data do not perfectly capture the OAS's or UNASUR's security governance labor. However, the

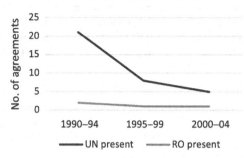

Figure 7 IGO presence at negotiations: Latin America and Caribbean

Figure 8 IGO facilitation of negotiations: Latin America and Caribbean

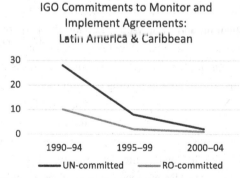

Figure 9 IGO commitments to monitor and implement agreements: Latin America and Caribbean

UN and African ROs also engage in security governance activities not captured by our data. We aim to be systematic in our IGO–IGO comparisons rather than comprehensive in our illumination of IGO governance work.

Table 2 Agreements engaged by LAC ROs and United Nations during
1990–2014

	# Agreements: IGO is present at negotiations	# Agreements: IGO facilitated negotiations	# Agreements: IGO commits to monitor and/or implement
United Nations	34	17	40
LAC ROs	4	3	16

Note: Some agreements were not engaged by any IGO, and some agreements were engaged by more than one IGO. See Online Appendix for methodology.
(Total number of agreements = 176)

2.4.2 Peace Missions

The OAS legitimized the US invasion of the Dominican Republic in 1965 by generating an Inter-American Force, and this is the only time the OAS (or any RO in the hemisphere) has used military force. As noted, the OAS lost relevance by the 1970s. The 1980s saw a resurgence of US unilateralism as well as LAC states turning to ad hoc regionalism (e.g. the Contadora Group) to address peace and security concerns. In the 1990s, the OAS again became a site for cooperation and norm promotion, and its security focus shifted from containment to interstate confidence building, the cooperative management of transnational security threats, and (especially) the defence of democracy.

The OAS also became involved in peace operations starting in the 1990s, taking on democracy and human rights promotion roles, but never deploying military units. Along with the UN it was included on the Commission for International Verification and Follow-up following the Esquipulas II process to end conflict in Central America. The OAS did not have the capacity to participate on par with the UN, but it did take on some tasks to complement the UN observer mission, including sending election monitors and later human rights monitors to Nicaragua (Baranyi 1995, 348–49). The Nicaraguan case "showed that the OAS would have to make significant investment in capacity building and norm development for engagement in peace operations" and resulted in greater UN leadership moving forward (Herz 2011, 51). For example, in El Salvador, the UN assumed the primary peacemaking and peace-building role, and the OAS monitored elections (Baranyi 1995, 254). The regional–global division of labor in the response to the 1991 Haiti coup proved more complicated. While the OAS initially took the lead – authorizing a civilian democracy-promotion mission, mediating talks, and sending an Inter-American Commission mission – the RO began to cede this leadership role to the UN in

1993 (Baranyi 1995, 359–60). At this point, a joint OAS–UN human rights mission was established to "receive communications about alleged human rights violations . . . to verify case follow-up in Haitian institutions . . . [and] to undertake public information and human rights education campaigns" ("International Civilian Support Mission in Haiti (MICAH)" n.d.) Soon thereafter, the UN escalated its intervention in the Haitian crisis, deploying the UN Mission in Haiti (1993) and later sending a series of military and police missions in 1996 and 1997 ("International Civilian Support Mission in Haiti (MICAH)" n.d.). The OAS did not partner with the UN in these missions.

As noted, the OAS has maintained a civilian peacebuilding mission in Colombia since 2004, and this is one of only two peace missions fielded by a LAC RO during 1990–2016 (see Figure 6). The UN does not have a military presence in Colombia, but it did begin fielding ceasefire verification missions starting in 2016, the most recent of which is tasked with "the verification of the reintegration of FARC-EP members into political, economic and social life; the implementation of personal and collective security and protection measures; and comprehensive security and protection programmes for communities and organizations in the territories" ("UN Verification Mission in Colombia" n.d.).

Overall, when looking at implementation of the fifteen peace missions deployed in the region during 1990–2016, we find that 60 percent (nine) were implemented by the UN, 26.6 percent (four) by individual states, and only 13.3 percent (two) were implemented by the OAS. None were implemented by an RO other than the OAS. Again, this does not mean that ROs do not engage in impactful security governance activities in LAC – but it does provide a clear contrast with the RO–UN division of labor in Africa.

One interesting recent development is the growing influence of international courts in LAC peace processes, particularly in Colombia. Both the ICC and Inter-American Court of Human Rights shaped the terms of the historic 2016 peace agreement – particularly on accountability – in meaningful ways. They did so through multiple avenues of influence, including "the threat of future litigation as well as the imprint of prior litigation" (Hillebrecht, Huneeus, and Borda 2018, 293) and "by providing discursive resources for [domestic] political actors to frame and advance political agendas" (Hillebrecht, Huneeus, and Borda 2018, 302). In this way, LAC IGOs are using a regional governance specialization – human rights governance – to intervene in peace and security.

3 Human Rights Governance

Human rights governance encompasses wide-ranging actors and activities. Inter-governmental organizations work to promote and protect human rights

Table 3 Categorizing regional and global human rights bodies

	State accountability model	Individual criminal accountability model
Quasi-judicial	UN treaty-monitoring bodies accepting petitions Inter-American Commission on Human Rights African Commission on Human and Peoples' Rights	
Judicial	Inter-American Court of Human Rights African Court on Human and Peoples' Rights	ICC

via standard setting, the solicitation and examination of state reports, the assessment of individual cases, in situ investigations and other fact-finding missions, special thematic rapporteurships, education campaigns, technical assistance, and even military intervention. This section zeros in on human rights accountability mechanisms, specifically IGO decision-making on individual cases or petitions. When it comes to human rights accountability, judicial and quasi-judicial bodies at the domestic, regional, and global levels follow one of two accountability models: state accountability or individual criminal accountability (Sikkink 2011, 13–14). State accountability mechanisms hold the state accountable for abuses by ruling on individual (or group) claims against the government and often ask or demand that the state compensate victims and/or make changes to domestic policy in response to findings of violation. Individual criminal accountability mechanisms hold individual agents of the state criminally accountable for abuses and can order prison sentences. Bodies of both types execute a human rights protection mandate, challenging state claims to exclusive jurisdiction over domestic affairs. The UN treaty-monitoring bodies, Inter-American Commission and African Commission on Human and Peoples' Rights are quasi-judicial, whereas the Inter-American Court, the African Court on Human and Peoples' Rights, and the ICC are judicial bodies.[13] With the exception of the ICC, all bodies under study here currently use a state accountability model, although this distinction is sometimes blurred when regional bodies order states to prosecute individual perpetrators. As

---

[13] This section generally excludes subregional human rights bodies, since they do not constitute "building blocks" of regional systems in the same way that the RECs are incorporated into APSA (see Section 2). However, we make note of one exceptional subregional body: the ECOWAS Court of Justice.

discussed in Section 3.1.2, the Inter-American Court in particular has carved out a robust "quasi-criminal" mandate for itself.

When it comes to human rights accountability, governance is highly regionalized in LAC, which is home to the trailblazing IAHRS. The IAHRS does not directly challenge the authority of the United Nations system (UNHRS) or ICC, but it is the more active and influential system in the region. While human rights governance in Africa is developing, the African human rights system (AfHRS) has yet to build the level of authority and ownership of its LAC counterpart. That said, human rights governance in one subregion – West Africa – is significantly more regionalized than the rest of the continent. To make this case, we compare the accountability mandates and activities of judicial and quasi-judicial bodies at the regional and global levels in LAC and in Africa. In line with this Element's overall analytical framework, we assess the degree of governance regionalization by investigating the global–regional distribution of authority (in terms of IGO legal mandates and policy influence) and the global–regional division of labor (in terms of recent petition and case workloads). When it comes to counting commission and court decisions, there is no central database, so we use the best available data source for each body. As specified in the Online Appendix, these sources range from annual reports (e.g. African Commission on Human and Peoples' Rights Activity Reports) to document search databases (e.g. OHCHR Jurisprudence Document Search) to multimedia statistical websites (e.g. IACHR Statistics).

3.1 Latin America and the Caribbean: The Authority Dimension of Governance

The LAC region has long-standing human rights frameworks.[14] The Ninth International Conference of American States adopted the American Declaration of the Rights and Duties of Man (American Declaration) in April 1948, and this instrument predates the UDHR. The American Declaration contains both civil and political rights, such as equality before the law and the right to life, as well as economic and social rights, such as the right to an education and the right to work and fair remuneration. It also encompasses individual duties, including the duty to vote, pay taxes, and serve the community and nation ("American Declaration of the Rights and Duties of Man" 1948). The Inter-American Commission was created in 1959 and gained authority to examine complaints related to specific human rights violations cases in 1965. The American Convention on Human Rights (ACHR), which

---

[14] Latin America and the Caribbean is defined as all Western hemisphere states excluding Canada, Guyana, Suriname, and the United States.

was adopted in 1969 and entered into force in 1978, defines human rights standards that state parties must follow. It also clarified the work of the Commission and established the Inter-American Court on Human Rights ("American Convention on Human Rights" 1978). The Court has been operating since 1979 and ruled on its first contentious case in 1988 (*Velasquez Rodriquez v. Honduras* 1988) ("Inter-American Human Rights System" n.d.). Together, the Inter-American Commission and Court constitute the IAHRS.

For the purposes of this section, the UNHRS refers to the eight treaty bodies that process individual petitions alleging state party violations of the relevant treaty. For example, the Human Rights Committee – which has been operating for decades – monitors compliance with the International Covenant on Civil and Political Rights (ICCPR) ("International Covenant on Civil and Political Rights" 1976). The ICC is a global-level court that began operating in 2002. It is to some degree autonomous from the UN. While there are other courts with universal jurisdictions, the UNHRS and ICC represent the global level of human rights governance for our purposes, as these are the only permanent bodies at the global level ruling on individual cases in the human rights domain ("International Courts" 2022).

The international human rights regime complex is nonhierarchical; no treaty identifies any IGO as having legal primacy vis-à-vis another IGO. This is different than the peace and security regime complex, since the UN Charter gives the global body primacy in matters of international peace and security. The elemental bodies of the human rights complex mostly work in parallel to one another, and global and regional legal accountability mandates significantly overlap. These mandates are not, however, identical; the formal jurisdiction of regional and global bodies varies with respect to which *states* are subject to which *procedures* concerning which *rights*. We can also identify variation across governance levels in the kind of legal authority, not just the degree of that authority – the Inter-American Court is the only human rights body (at the regional or global level) with the power to issue binding decisions against LAC states, whereas the ICC is the only IGO with the power to prosecute individuals in the Americas. This variation contributes to a de jure state accountability-criminal accountability division of labor, but this division is less clear in practice. Finally, the Inter-American Court's greater influence relative to the UNHRS and ICC is evidenced by the intrusiveness of its measures as well as its embeddedness in domestic legal systems, facilitated in part by the doctrine of conventionality control, which holds that "domestic courts were obliged not to apply national norms which were in violation of the ACHR and, what is more, in the interpretation given to the Convention by the Inter-American Court" (Binder 2012, 307).

3.1.1 Quasi-Judicial Bodies

At first glance, the Inter-American Commission and the UN treaty-monitoring bodies share strikingly similar individual petitions mandates: they are empowered to receive petitions directly from individuals; they review these petitions and issue nonbinding decisions (or "views"); in some cases, precautionary measures may be issued to prevent imminent violations; follow-up procedures facilitate some monitoring of state compliance with decisions and compliance records published via official reports; and most bodies conduct some fact-finding country visits (see "Individual Communications" n.d.; "Inter-American Human Rights System" n.d.).

However, the Inter-American Commission's petition mandate is more authoritative than those of the UN bodies, due to (1) the breadth of rights covered in the Inter-American legal instruments and (2) the Inter-American Commission's automatic jurisdiction over all states in the region. Individuals and groups submitting petitions to the Inter-American Commission must allege a violation of the American Declaration or, if the relevant state has ratified it, to the ACHR.[15] Both documents cover a broad range of civil, political, economic, and social rights, whereas each UN treaty body monitors only a subset of rights (those outlined in the specific treaty).

All thirty-one LAC states are subject to the individual communications procedures of the Inter-American Commission. In the UNHRS, there is significant variation across treaty bodies in the extent to which LAC states are actually subject to the petition procedures of the UNHRS (see Table 4). The UN treaty bodies, which are also composed of experts, may receive and issue views on a communication only if the relevant state is party to an optional protocol (e.g. First Optional Protocol to the ICCPR) or has made a declaration (e.g. under Article 14 of the International Convention on the Elimination of All Forms of Racial Discrimination), depending on the treaty. So, in order to be subject to this procedure, a state must not only ratify the relevant treaty but must also elect to separately recognize competence of the relevant committee.

3.1.2 Judicial Bodies

The Inter-American Court and the ICC are both judicial bodies – the former issues judgments against states on wide-ranging violations and the latter prosecutes individuals on a narrow set of international crimes, including genocide, crimes against humanity, and war crimes. A key distinguishing feature of the

---

[15] In other words, there is a two-track system (depending on an individual state's status vis-à-vis the ACHR).

Table 4 States subject to petitions procedures in LAC

Quasi-judicial body	# States subject to petitions procedure as of October 7, 2022
Inter-American Commission	31
*UN treaty-monitoring bodies**	
Human Rights Committee	20
Committee on the Rights of Persons with Disabilities	20
Committee on the Elimination of Discrimination against Women	18
Committee Against Torture	13
Committee on the Elimination of Racial Discrimination	12 .
Committee on the Rights of the Child	11
Committee on Economic, Social, and Cultural Rights	7
Committee on Enforced Disappearances	4

* **Source:** United Nations Human Rights Office of the High Commissioner, "Status of Ratification Interactive Dashboard." https://indicators.ohchr.org.

IAHRS that makes it significantly more authoritative than the UNHRS is the binding nature of the Inter-American Court's judgments. The Inter-American Commission's decisions are nonbinding, but it has the power to refer cases up to the Court – and the UN treaty bodies lack this power of referral. The UN bodies issue "views" rather than judgments, and they are staffed with "experts" rather than judges. International legal scholars debate the legal status of quasi-judicial views (Ulfstein 2012, 92–100). States have been known to justify their own noncompliance with reference to these decisions' nonbinding nature (van Alebeek and Nollkaemper 2012). In light of this and other limitations of the current UN system, proposals for a "World Court of Human Rights" have been put forward (Nowak 2007) – but such a major reform does not appear likely in the near future (Ulfstein 2012, 105).[16] When it comes to state accountability for violations, then, the regional system is considerably more authoritative than the global system in LAC.

When it comes to individual criminal accountability, the question of the regional–global distribution of authority is less straightforward. To be sure,

---

[16] See also the World Court of Human Rights Development Project: www.worldcourtofhumanrights.net/home.

the ICC is the only international criminal law court with jurisdiction in the Americas. Based strictly on their legal mandates, we can see a division of labor between the individual criminal accountability activities of the global judicial body operating in the Americas and the state accountability activities of the regional judicial body operating in the Americas. However, as explained in this section, this division is muddied in practice as a result of the Inter-American Court's "quasi-criminal" review activities.

The authority of the Inter-American Court is based on the ACHR. In order to be subject to its contentious jurisdiction, a state must ratify the Convention and must also separately recognize the Court's competence. The Inter-American Court considers cases referred to it by the Inter-American Commission or by a state party to the ACHR. In order for a case to be admissible to the Inter-American Commission (and by extension, to the Court), domestic remedies must be exhausted by the petitioner. The ICC is much newer – it has been operating since 2002, when the Rome Statute entered into force. In order for the ICC to have jurisdiction in a case, the crime in question must have been committed in the territory of a state party or have been perpetrated by a state party national. Alternatively, the UNSC may refer cases to the ICC ("Rome Statute of the International Criminal Court" 2002). The ICC operates according to the principle of complementarity, which is somewhat comparable to the domestic exhaustion requirement of the IAHRS; the ICC can only initiate cases when the domestic judicial system is unwilling or unable to proceed.

As of 2022, nineteen LAC states accept the Inter-American Court's contentious jurisdiction ("What Is the I/A Court H.R.?" n.d.) and twenty-six LAC states are party to the Rome Statute, making them subject to the ICC jurisdiction ("Assembly of States Parties to the Rome Statute" n.d.). This means that the global court has greater geographical reach in the region. However, the Inter-American Court has a more expansive jurisdiction with respect to the rights it oversees (those outlined in the ACHR), as the ICC can only prosecute major atrocity crimes.

The ICC's international legal monopoly on criminal matters is undercut by the Inter-American Court's engagement in "quasi-criminal" review (Huneeus 2013). The regional court's focus on atrocity crimes and criminal justice, and its significant involvement in prosecutorial processes, sets it apart from other human rights bodies. As Huneeus (2018) explains:

> Although it is not a criminal court, the Inter-American Court typically orders states to prosecute as a remedial measure. It is the only human rights court to do so. Further, it has interpreted its powers to include the ability to monitor

compliance to its orders, which means that it becomes involved in monitoring the advance of domestic criminal investigations. . . . Throughout the judgment and compliance phases, the Court is not shy of delving into criminal files and opining on differing aspects of the criminal investigation, including advising prosecutors to interrogate specific witnesses and to investigate particular theories of the case. (Huneeus 2018, 121–22)

Several landmark IAHRS cases address the domestic amnesty problem. In *Velasquez Rodriquez* v. *Honduras* (1988), the Court found that states have an obligation to "investigate, prosecute, punish, and repair grave human rights violations" (Roht-Arriaza 2019, 4). Another seminal case in transitional justice jurisprudence, *Barrios Altos* v. *Peru* (2001), pertained to massacres carried out in the early 1990s. These massacres had been ordered by Alberto Fujimori, the sitting president at the time of the case's consideration by the Court. Amnesty laws passed in 1995 by the Fujimori government shielded Fujimori and others responsible for the atrocities. The Inter-American Court found that these laws violated the rights of victims and families to judicial recourse and contributed to impunity, contrary to the spirit of the ACHR. As such, the Court found that these amnesty laws were "devoid of legal effects" (Binder 2012, 303–4). The judgment states:

> Owing to the manifest incompatibility of self-amnesty laws and the American Convention on Human Rights, the said laws lack legal effect and may not continue to obstruct the investigation of the grounds on which this case is based or the identification and punishment of those responsible, nor can they have the same or a similar impact with regard to other cases that have occurred in Peru, where the rights established in the American Convention have been violated. (*Barrios Altos* v. *Peru* 2001, 14)

Peru's domestic legal system makes it possible to give effect to international court decisions. The Peruvian Constitutional Court found that the Inter-American Court's judgment was binding and ordered that Peru comply with the Barrios Altos decision. This culminated in the 2009 conviction of Fujimori by the Special Criminal Court Chamber of the Peruvian Supreme Court for the Barrios Altos and La Cantuta massacres. He was sentenced to twenty-five years in prison (Binder 2012, 315). In this case, Peru fully complied, and this can be seen as a powerful example of member state's acceptance of the Inter-American Court's authority. Although not universally, many other states in the region have implemented the anti-impunity norm championed by the Court. Latin America has seen many prosecutions for past atrocities, including in Argentina, Chile, and Guatemala. El Salvador was late to comply and only annulled its amnesty laws in 2016 with a few cases now slowly proceeding, and Brazil is also reluctant to pursue prosecutions (Roht-Arriaza 2019, 5). There have also been concerns about the Court's legitimacy – some scholars argue that it prioritizes human rights standards over democratic accountability (Perez-Leon-Acevedo 2020, 683). This of course represents contestation of the Court's authority.

Other indicators of the impressive influence of the IAHRS include the intrusiveness of its remedies and its embeddedness in domestic legal systems. According to Huneeus (2015), the Inter-American Court stands out for its "structural" rulings which require the state "to reform or create a bureaucracy or policy" (Huneeus 2015, 10). Antkowiak adds that "The Inter-American Court is the primary international body to redress serious human rights violations and international crimes with not only compensation, but also equitable remedies such as restitution and rehabilitation" (Antkowiak 2008, 415). Related to the intrusiveness of remedies is another indicator of authority: the degree to which the work of the IGO is "embedded" in domestic legal systems. Indeed, Hunneeus and Madsen argue that what sets regional human rights bodies apart from global human rights bodies is the former's embeddedness. Regional bodies have "come to engage in increasingly dense interactions with domestic courts, becoming far more deeply embedded in national systems than the UN system" (Huneeus and Madsen 2018, 137). The European and Inter-American courts in particular have begun "to take on attributes typically associated with national constitutional courts" and have become "more deeply embedded in the domestic legal realm, so that [their] influence was felt not only through international litigation but also through the daily decisions of domestic judges and other state actors, and even non-state actors, who made reference to the regional case law as an authoritative guide" (Huneeus and Madsen 2018, 151).

The Inter-American Court has encouraged this embeddedness through its establishment of the doctrine of conventionality control, which has sought to mandate domestic judges to enforce its interpretation of the ACHR. The doctrine originated with the 2006 *Almonacid* v. *Chile* case pertaining to a 1973 extrajudicial killing by state forces during the Pinochet regime. The Court found that as this was a crime against humanity, it must be prosecuted, voiding a 1978 amnesty decree law. The ruling went further than previous rulings and established for the first time the doctrine of conventionality control (Binder 2012, 304–5). It obliged domestic courts to apply the Inter-American Court interpretation of the ACHR and not domestic norms (Binder 2012, 307). Thus the Court sought to ascribe immense authority to itself as the sole arbiter of the evolving nature of the interpretation of the ACHR. Furthermore, Inter-American Court's jurisprudence holds that domestic courts or authorities do not need to amend or repeal legislation, such as amnesty laws, that are in violation of the ACHR. If the Inter-American Court finds that laws are without legal effect, then there is no further action that is needed for its decision to be applied in domestic jurisdictions. In

essence, "the Inter-American Court attributes supranational force to its determin-
ations and acts like a domestic constitutional court" (Binder 2012, 306–7).

3.2 Latin America and the Caribbean: The Ownership Dimension of Governance

In addition to its greater legal authority and influence, the regional system is also
more active than the global system. It does more human rights governance
"work" with respect to individual cases.

3.2.1 Quasi-Judicial Workloads

The IAHRS has a greater caseload than the UNHRS. During the 2010–
20 period, the eight relevant UN treaty bodies together issued forty-six decisions on the merits (in regard to communications from LAC countries). During
that same period, the Inter-American Commission approved 307 merits reports
on LAC cases. In other words, the IAHRS issued six to seven times more
decisions on merits than did the UNHRS during these years.

An individual cannot submit the same complaint to both a UN body and to
a regional body,[17] so complainants must choose whether to "go regional" or "go
global." Several factors likely jointly account for the greater regional caseload. First,
all OAS member states are subject to the individual petition procedures of the
IAHRS, but the same is not true for the UNHRS (see Table 3). Given this, we would
expect the regional body's caseload to be higher, although not *six times* higher.
Second, some of the UN treaty bodies have only recently acquired the power to
receive individual complaints and are not yet as established as the IAHRS. Third,
and relatedly, the IAHRS may simply be more visible (than the UNHRS) to
individuals and nongovernmental organizations (NGOs) in the region. Writing
over twenty years ago, Pinto observed that the Human Rights Committee "has
never enjoyed the publicity of the [Inter-American Commission] in the countries of
the western hemisphere" (Pinto 1999, 841). More recently, a UN Secretary-General
report suggested that "Regional and subregional mechanisms, which are located
geographically closer to the complainant, may be more visible and considered more
approachable by the complainant. This could particularly be the case for complainants who lack the resources to direct their case to the international system" ("Report
of the Secretary-General on the Workshop on Regional Arrangements for the
Promotion and Protection of Human Rights, 24 and 25 November 2008" 2009)

---

[17] According to the OHCHR website, "If [the same matter] has been submitted to another treaty
body or to a regional ... the Committees cannot examine the complaint. The aim of this rule is to
avoid unnecessary duplication at the international level." www.ohchr.org/EN/HRBodies/
TBPetitions/Pages/IndividualCommunications.aspx.

Finally, Engstrom and Low draw on interview data to suggest that, at least in some cases, litigants prefer to take their petitions to the IAHRS because it is more convenient and because "gaining a binding ruling from the Inter-American Court was also a potential outcome that was not available in the UN system" (Engstrom and Low 2019, 39). This suggests that the greater *authority* of the Inter-American system contributes to its greater *ownership* of human rights governance. This is another example, then, of how authority and ownership feed into one another (the first example being that regional ownership has contributed to regional authority in African peace process engagement – see Section 2).

3.2.2 Judicial Workloads

No ICC cases have ever been initiated in the Americas. All ICC cases to date address crimes in Africa. By contrast, from 2002 (when the ICC began operations) to 2019, the Inter-American Commission sent 270 cases to the Inter-American Court ("Inter-American Commission on Human Rights: Statistics" n.d.). The Inter-American Court's caseload increased threefold in the 2000s (compared to the 1990s), pursuant to the 2001 reform of the Rules of Procedure of the Inter-American Commission. This is to some degree comparing apples to oranges, but it is nevertheless the case that there is *more judicial activity happening at the regional level* than at the global level. And there is no global body with the power to hold states legally accountable for human rights violations in the region (only individuals). As Huneeus and Madsen (2018) note, while most scholars focus on the UN-based system, "It is nevertheless the regional systems where much – if not most – of the human rights action has unfolded, and not only in recent years but from the very beginning. Most decisively, the regional systems have developed judicial institutions that render binding judgments on member states" (Huneeus and Madsen 2018, 137).

Although the ICC has not actually prosecuted any cases in the Americas, as of 2022 it has one "Situation Under Investigation" in Venezuela. It has also opened "Preliminary Examinations" in four cases: Colombia (since June 2004), Venezuela I (since February 2018), Venezuela II (since February 2020), and Bolivia (since September 2020) ("Cases" n.d.).[18] These Examinations put the ICC in the position to exert influence on domestic processes. The threat of prosecution is a lever of influence that the ICC possesses, and this is something the Inter-American Court lacks. Still, "the ICC is not yet as deeply embedded in the domestic judicial system" as the IAHRS (Huneeus 2018, 127). These bodies bring different governance tools to the problem of impunity.

---

[18] It has since closed examinations in Bolivia, Colombia, and Honduras and promoted the Venezuela I case to a "situation under investigation." See Online Appendix.

3.3 Africa: The Authority Dimension of Governance

Human rights governance is less regionalized in Africa than in LAC,[19] but that does not mean that the region has not made strides in human rights governance. The African Court has made moves to expand its authority, and it boasts innovative mandates, but its limited functionality undermines its ability to take fuller ownership over human rights tasks. In West Africa, the ECOWAS Court of Justice stands out for its own innovative mandate and relatively large caseload.

The African regional community has historically made important contributions to international human rights norms although these initiatives were sometimes distinct from the work of the AfHRS. For example, Article I of the UDHR establishes that human beings are endowed with equal dignity and rights, and Article II prohibits discrimination on the basis of several protected characteristics, including race ("Universal Declaration of Human Rights" 1948). However, these articles were typically applied to individuals and not state behavior, with internal affairs of states being protected by sovereignty norms. African states challenged this interpretation of these human rights norms, and the Lusaka Manifesto, endorsed by the OAU, argues for distinct consequences for racialized oppression:

> The Republic of South Africa is itself an independent sovereign state and a Member of the United Nations. ... On every legal basis its internal affairs are a matter exclusively for the people of South Africa. Yet the purpose of law is people and we assert that the actions of the South African Government are such that the rest of the world has a responsibility to take some action in defence of humanity. ("The Lusaka Manifesto on Southern Africa Proclaimed by the Fifth Summit Conference of East and Central African States" 1969)

African states, institutions, and communities have also challenged many legalistic transitional justice norms and implemented transitional justice practices rooted in local frameworks (Murithi 2018, 161). The most well-known example of transitional justice from Africa may be South Africa's process following the end of apartheid that prioritized a restorative justice model but with sequencing that allowed space for both retributive and restorative processes (Murithi 2018, 164).

Returning to the more formalized AfHRS, this system dates back several decades, and has evolved and grown over time. As discussed in Section 2, the OAU was created in 1963 and was not primarily concerned with a broad conception of human rights. The African Charter on Human and Peoples' Rights (Banjul Charter) was not adopted and ratified until the 1980s. All AU

---

[19] Africa includes sub-Saharan Africa and North Africa.

member states except Morocco are party to the Banjul Charter, which was adopted in 1981 and entered into force in 1986, while the Commission was established in November 1987 ("Important Dates" n.d.). The Charter establishes not only rights and freedoms of individuals but also their duties toward family, community, and society. It also established the Commission to promote and research Human and Peoples' Rights, conduct investigations, set out principles to resolve legal and legislative issues around rights, ensure the protection of rights, and interpret the rights set out in the Charter ("African (Banjul) Charter on Human and Peoples' Rights" 1986). The state parties to the Charter are subject to the African Commission's individual petition procedure, which is similar to that of the Inter-American Commission ("Communications Procedure" n.d.).

As in Latin America and the Caribbean, more African states are subject to the petitions procedures of the African Commission than to that of the UN treaty-monitoring bodies (see Table 5).

Table 5 States subject to petitions procedures in Africa

Quasi-judicial body	# States subject to petitions procedure as of October 7, 2022
African Commission on Human and Peoples' Rights*	54
*UN treaty-monitoring bodies***	
Human Rights Committee	36
Committee on the Rights of Persons with Disabilities	25
Committee on the Elimination of Discrimination against Women	29
Committee Against Torture	9
Committee on the Elimination of Racial Discrimination	5
Committee on the Rights of the Child	4
Committee on Economic, Social, and Cultural Rights	1
Committee on Enforced Disappearances	1

* *Source:* African Commission on Human and Peoples' Rights, "Statistics." www.achpr.org/statistics.

** *Source:* United Nations Human Rights Office of the High Commissioner, "Status of Ratification Interactive Dashboard." https://indicators.ohchr.org.

The African Court was established through a 1998 Protocol to the Banjul Charter (the Protocol), which entered into force in 2004. The jurisdiction of the African Court as defined in its constitutive document is unique in that it can apply any human rights instrument ratified by the state concerned (not just regional instruments) ("Protocol to the African Charter on Human and Peoples' Rights on the Establishment of an African Court on Human and Peoples' Rights" 2004). The parameters of what exactly constitutes a human rights treaty are not rigidly defined. Thus far the Court has reviewed alleged violations of several treaties across levels of governance, including the ICCPR, ECOWAS Revised Treaty, African Charter on Democracy, and Convention on the Elimination of All Forms of Discrimination Against Women, among others (Rachovitsa 2019, 268). The Court's jurisdiction over any human rights treaty ratified by State parties means that it "consolidates human rights obligations of States parties under the auspices of a single judicial body on a regional level" (Rachovitsa 2019, 273–74). There are of course legitimate reasons to be wary of consolidation, and the ACtHPR is currently weak. However, that does not take away from the fact that the ACtHPR was created with a unique jurisdiction and has continued to develop and reinforce that jurisdiction through its jurisprudence. There is therefore potential for the AfHRS to indirectly challenge the centrality of the UNHRS. As Rachovitsa notes:

> The authority of regional bodies to construe international law brings to the fore informal hierarchies among said international courts, and the structural imbalance entrenched in the Euro-centred map of the international law landscape. ... The "law of Geneva" and the "law of the Hague" assign international law a location, and narrate a specific story of progress. This inhibits us from giving due regard to the seemingly unlikely places in which international law may be found. The ACtHPR can be seen as part of a different plausible map of international law. (Rachovitsa 2019, 279)

Like the Inter-American Court, the ACtHPR has in practice exercised a "quasi-criminal" jurisdiction, although to a lesser extent than its Inter-American counterpart (Viljoen 2019, 318). Furthermore, as is well documented elsewhere, the AU has presented a multidimensional challenge to the ICC's authority on the continent (Boehme 2017). One development that can be understood as part of this challenge is the 2014 adoption by the AU Assembly of the Malabo Protocol, which will – if and when it enters into force – expand the African Court's jurisdiction to include criminal cases ("Protocol on Amendments to the Protocol on the Statute of the African Court of Justice and Human Rights" Not in force). This prospect certainly raises questions about future conflict and competition between regional and global criminal courts. That said, Abebe's (2017) analysis of the actual jurisdictional overlap (or lack thereof) between the proposed chamber and the ICC suggests that a relatively neat division of labor is possible. Most importantly, the ICC prioritizes the prosecution of "big fish" like state leaders, whereas the Malabo Protocol provides immunity to state officials while they are in office (Abebe 2017). Furthermore, entry into force is likely not imminent – no state has yet ratified the Protocol ("Status List: Protoco on Amendments to the Protocol on the Statute of the African Court of Justice and Human Rights" 2019). However, it is important to acknowledge the Malabo Protocol because the proposed Court's jurisdiction would include not only human rights but also general international law and international criminal law, which would be unprecedented (Murray 2019, 975). The judicial landscape of African regional courts will continue to evolve. This section does not offer a comprehensive overview of all reform attempts and our data focuses on the ACtHPR that is currently operational. Despite high-profile African state pushback against the ICC and the potential for a new African court to emerge, thirty-three AU members remain states parties to the Rome Statute ("Assembly of States Parties to the Rome Statute" n.d.). When it comes to the ACtHPR, as of 2022, thirty-three African states have ratified the Protocol establishing the Court, but only six states accept the competence of the Court to hear cases filed directly by individuals and NGOs (rather than referred by the Commission) ("Basic Information" n.d.).

Even with the existing structures, the AfHRS is younger than the IAHRS and has therefore had less time to develop its jurisprudence and exert influence on state behavior and on the workings of domestic courts. According to Huneeus and Madsen, the African system is less embedded in national legal systems than are the Inter-American and European systems (Huneeus and Madsen 2018, 151). Viljoen suggests that the African system might take inspiration from the development of the more established Inter-American Court's "elaborate compliance practice"[20] as well as from the Inter-American Commission's "much more extensive" use of interim (i.e. precautionary or urgent) measures with their specific – rather than vague – recommendations (Viljoen 2019, 310). We therefore argue that human rights authority is currently less regionalized (and still in flux) in Africa than in the LAC region, since authority of the UN treaty-monitoring bodies is comparable in the two regions and the ICC has asserted more authority in Africa via prosecutorial activity.

Unlike in the peace and security domain where the RECs form part of the APSA, subregional courts are not integrated into the continental AfHRS. However, it is worth making note of one particular subregional judicial body –

---

[20] This practice includes "comprehensive and continuous engagement, public compliance hearings and separate judgements on the issue of compliance" (Viljoen 2019, 306–7).

the ECOWAS Court of Justice – which acquired human rights jurisdiction in 2005 and boasts of "strikingly capacious jurisdiction and access rules" (Alter, Helfer, and McAllister 2013, 738), including the right of complainants to bring cases without first exhausting domestic remedies. There is no ECOWAS human rights commission, so complainants bring cases directly to the court. By contrast, the other judicial and quasi-judicial bodies under review in this section require local remedy exhaustion. The ECOWAS Court has ruled on several high-profile cases during its first seventeen years. In a landmark 2008 case, it held Niger responsible for failing to protect a woman from enslavement, ordering the government to pay the equivalent of $19,000 in reparations to Hadijatou Mani (Polgreen 2008). More recently, the ECOWAS Court has engendered what Akinkugbe terms the "judicialization of mega-politics" in West Africa by using its human rights jurisdiction to weigh in on electoral disputes (Akinkugbe 2020).

3.4 Africa: The Ownership Dimension of Governance

Compared to the Inter-American Commission, the African Commission is "highly underused" (Huneeus and Madsen 2018, 150). In their study on victim access to regional human rights bodies, Hampson, Martin, and Viljoen (2018) refer to the caseload of the AfHRS as "unacceptably low."[21] During the 2012–20 period, the eight relevant UN treaty bodies together issued ninety-four views (in regard to communications from African countries). During that same period, the African Commission issued forty-six decisions. These totals include one unusual year – 2014 – when the UN bodies issued thirty views, which is considerably higher than any other year under review. If we exclude 2014, these totals drop to sixty-six (UN bodies) and forty-one (African Commission).[22]

When it comes to judicial bodies at the global level, the high-profile ICC is almost solely focused on the African continent. All thirty cases are associated with situations on the continent (although there are ongoing investigations and preliminary examinations elsewhere).[23] The African Court on Human and Peoples' Rights has only been issuing rulings since 2009, handing down its first judgment on the

---

[21] Hampson, Martin, and Viljoen (2018) explain this low caseload (compared to other regional systems including the IAHRS) as the result of "major impediments to ... legal recourse" at the *domestic level*. "[T]he overwhelming majority of people in Africa have no real access to the African machinery for a variety of reasons that have nothing to do with the admissibility provisions" of the African regional bodies (185). It stands to reason that this phenomenon affects the UNHRS workload in kind.

[22] Interestingly, about two-thirds of the African cases decided by a UN body pertains to North Africa specifically (Algeria, Libya, Morocco, or Tunisia). In 2014, for example, twenty-three of the twenty-nine cases decided by the UN bodies pertained to Algeria (fourteen), Libya (five), or Morocco (four).

[23] See this Element's Online Appendix for details.

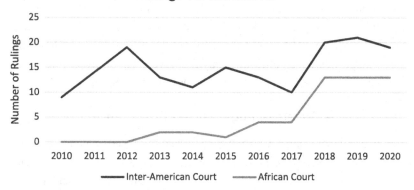

Figure 10 Regional human rights courts: Rulings on the merits

merits in 2013. Only very recently (2018–20) has its number of merits rulings entered the double digits (see Figure 10). We find that it is currently less active than the Inter-American Court, although comparing caseloads across regional courts is difficult since regions vary in size, both in terms of the number of RO member states and the total human population living therein. The OAS has thirty-one LAC member states, and the total population of LAC was around 652 million in 2020 ("Population, Total – Latin American and Caribbean" n.d.). The AU has fifty-five member states, and sub-Saharan Africa alone had a population of 1.1 billion in 2020 ("Population, Total – Sub-Saharan Africa" n.d.). The geographic distribution of the African Court rulings is worthy of note: for thirty-nine out of the fifty-eight rulings visualized above (67 percent), the respondent state was Tanzania. Inter-American Court rulings were considerably more spread out during this period. The ECOWAS Court has meanwhile been highly active on human rights cases, considering it was only empowered to hear such cases seventeen years ago. Again, ECOWAS does not have a human rights commission (a quasi-judicial body), so its only merits decisions are Court decisions. During 2016–20, it issued seventy-three rulings on the merits for cases involving allegations of human rights violations, which is high relative to other bodies studied here given that ECOWAS only has fifteen member states. Only four of the ICC's thirty cases are associated with situations in West Africa (Côte d'Ivoire and Mali).

The future of the ACtHPR is unclear. On the one hand, there has been a decline in the number of states accepting its jurisdiction to hear cases brought directly by individuals, leading one observer to predict that "the court will soon simply run out of cases" (Sandner 2020). And the establishment of the proposed criminal chamber seems far-off. On the other hand, the caseload of the Court has increased rather significantly over its first several years. As Daly and Wiebusch (2018) argue, this record is impressive relative to that of the Inter-American Court during its first decade. Furthermore, "the African Court has found rights violations in every merits judgment issued, unlike its European and Inter-American counterparts' first-decade jurisprudence. Crucially . . . many of the Court's judgments have struck at highly sensitive areas of public policy, the constitutional order, and state power . . . " (Daly and Wiebusch 2018, 297–98).

4 Drivers of Regionalized Governance

States in the Global South have many good reasons to cooperate and build institutions at the regional level as opposed to – or in addition to – the global level. Anti-colonial macronational movements, like Pan-Africanism, organized and agitated well before the UN was created, establishing the discursive and networking foundations for the creation of ROs. Formal regionalism in the form of the Pan-American Union predates the UN by decades, and Latin American delegates at the UN's founding lobbied against UN primacy vis-à-vis ROs. Regionalism, then, is not a secondary alternative to globalism. Global institutions do often boast wider reach and deeper resources, but this does not necessarily make them the better governance alternative, for a wide variety of reasons. As Acharya (2016b) argues, regionalism in the Global South can serve states in their struggle for autonomy from great power influence and intervention in ways that the UN cannot. Relatedly, regional interventions may boast greater legitimacy in the eyes of stakeholders than will extraregional interventions spearheaded by former colonial powers. At the UN, power is not concentrated in the General Assembly but rather in the Security Council where the Permanent Five wield their vetoes. The flip side of this is UN weakness and neglect of Global South concerns. In the domain of conflict management, ROs in Africa have proved more willing and able than the UN to deploy to conflict situations where there is not yet peace to keep. That said regional institutions are not simply a response to undemocratic or weak UN institutions. They develop to solve regional problems and/or in the name of regional values – in parallel with or even ahead of global institutions. In some instances regional institutions ultimately become more effective or influential. A prime example is the IAHRS system which did not arise to challenge the UN system; it works in parallel to its global counterpart, building on decades of its own precedents.

But why, then, is the regionalization of governance in the Global South uneven? More specifically for our purposes, why does Africa specialize in peace and security governance while LAC specializes in human rights accountability governance? In this section, we theorize divergent regional institutional development with an emphasis on regional agency. The phenomenon of regional "specialties" suggests regional – rather than global or extraregional – drivers. While the global proliferation of regional institutions working in these issue areas might prompt us to turn to theories of diffusion (Risse 2016) and localization (Acharya 2004), these approaches come up short in analyses of regional governance specialization. While some specialties diffuse to other regions or the global arena, others do not, and their development is not best understood as the product of a "localized" global script. Before presenting our explanatory framework and applying it to these cases, we first outline our underlying assumptions and commitments.

4.1 Assumptions and Commitments

First, we are persuaded by scholarship that rejects the relevance of the EU integration model to analysis of regionalism outside Europe. As Börzel and Risse (2019) observe, the EU is the only case where we see high economic interdependence and strong regionalism. "Sub-Saharan Africa and Latin America show low interdependence with strong regionalism while North America and East Asia present the opposite of high economic interdependence and low regionalism" (Börzel and Risse 2019, 1232). According to Acharya (2016b), while the logic of regionalism in the EU context is integration, the logic of postcolonial regionalism is more often autonomy (especially autonomy from extraregional influence and intervention) (Acharya 2016b). He further argues that "the EU model has not and will not travel well in the developing world" (Acharya 2016b, 110). Mumford (2020) draws out the normative implications of this misapplication, writing that EU-centric comparative regionalism "helps to craft a narrative of homogenous problems" and "risks constructing the various regions as problems in themselves (i.e. failing integration efforts, poor mimics, layers of 'decoupled' institutions) that require solutions through the intervention of European counterparts" (Mumford 2020).

Regional integration schemes should not be seen as "region-free" global norms but rather a European innovation that responds to context-specific needs and could *potentially* be applied in other regions. European integration is a regional preference and conflict resolution tool. Out of the ashes of two world wars and numerous intra-European wars in the preceding centuries, Europe pooled sovereignty in order to alter "elite perceptions of the structural conditions within which they exercised and/or competed for power" (Stefanova 2006, 86). Integration as a conflict resolution strategy has been used throughout the developmental phases of the EU. After the end of the Cold War the EU enacted a policy of enlargement to bring in Eastern European states in order to enhance security and stability for the whole of Europe (Stefanova 2006, 90). The EU was also engaged in third-party mediation in the conflict in the former Yugoslavia. The atrocities in this conflict are well documented as is the European failure to address the violence. However, in the aftermath, and in line with the European norm of integration, the EU adopted a policy of "Europeanization" that links the outcome of a conflict resolution process with the extent to which parties to the conflict can be brought into European structures. As Stefanova argues, "it replicates the original model of conflict resolution in post-World War II Western Europe by restructuring a postconflict environment into a regional framework, common incentive structures, and standards of acceptable behavior" (Stefanova 2006, 90).

We echo calls from the Third World Approaches to International Law literature for greater recognition of peripheral international legal histories (Obregón 2019) as well as critiques of the "implicit Eurocentrism" of works that portray "ideas and norms that originated in Europe" as "somehow region-free," while "concepts and interpretations that originated elsewhere are geographical and cultural variations, even aberrations" (Kirmse 2014, 311). We do not take EU regionalism as a key point of reference when seeking to explain governance regionalization in Africa and LAC, nor do we take integration as an endpoint of regionalism.

Second and relatedly, we emphasize the value of South–South comparison within comparative regionalism, because of common albeit distinct colonial histories. Systematic and direct comparison between and among these regions offers great explanatory leverage. It illuminates things that are otherwise obscured. For example, if we are only analyzing ASEAN "on its own terms," we might attribute its strong nonintervention norm to the postcolonial experience (as many have). But other postcolonial ROs – like the AU – are much more interventionist than ASEAN (Coe 2015). Comparison pushes us to dig deeper when explaining outcomes. In the same vein, since both the OAS and AU have developed human rights bodies and peace and security institutions, we can say that these issue areas are regionalized to some degree in both regions. We might attribute this phenomenon to diffusion. But once we compare the extent of regionalization in the two regions and issue areas, as we do in this Element, we can see how much more regionalized human rights is in LAC and how much more regionalized peace and security is in Africa.

By comparing regions in the Global South, we do not seek to derive parsimonious grand theory. While we find Acharya's distinction between the integration and autonomy logics of regionalism to be useful to some degree, his analysis overstates the attachment of postcolonial states to nonintervention norms (Acharya 2016b). This is actually a key point of variation, as ASEAN's steadfast commitment to nonintervention makes Southeast Asia an outlier rather than an exemplar in the Global South, especially when compared to Africa and the LAC region (Coe 2015). Comparison draws out important variation across the Global South and allows us to avoid exaggerating the similarities across these regions. Further South–South comparison should also encourage scholars to truly compare regions without using the EU as a yard stick for RO performance and effectiveness.

Third, while we do not dismiss diffusion theory – which theorizes processes of interdependent policymaking (Risse 2016) – we do find its explanatory power to be limited when it comes to understanding the variation we observe across regions in this Element. As others have pointed out, institutional diffusion is often superficial. In their study of supposed similarities between the EU and AU, for example, Fioramonti and Mattheis (2016) find that:

> Both regions have adopted the word "union." Both are led by a Commission, some type of Council/s and a regional Parliament. They even have a similar flag, with the maps of the respective continents surrounded by a circle of stars. Europe and Africa, through their "twin" organizations, have been made closer – but only apparently so. When one looks at the actual drivers, approaches, principles and modalities of regionalization, it becomes clear that neither Europe nor Africa followed clearly defined linear paths to integration, and that differences are certainly more significant than superficial similarities. (Fioramonti and Mattheis 2016, 686)

According to Risse's overview of the state of the art of diffusion scholarship (2016), "most empirical work [on diffusion] is still rather Euro- and Western-centric, despite all pledges to the contrary" (Risse 2016, 102). Some authors have sought to bring more (Global South) agency to diffusion theory. Acharya has proposed the notion of norm localization wherein regions adapt international norms through a number of mechanisms to fit local needs (Acharya 2004). Localization echoes Merry's concept of discourse "vernacularization," which she uses to theorize the dynamics of the human rights movement (Merry 2006). Meanwhile, Williams applies localization theory to African regional security governance (Williams 2007). Even when exploring the agency of local or regional actors, the focus often seems to be on contestation rather than origination. For example, Zimmermann and colleagues argue that contestation is a form of normative agency (Zimmermann, Deitelhoff, and Lesch 2017). Our findings indicate that regions develop specializations, so diffusion of international norms is an inadequate explanation for varying levels of governance regionalization.

Finally, we seek to build on work that illuminates the agency and protagonism of actors in the Global South, examining their normative innovations and impact on the evolution of global governance (Coleman and Tieku 2018; Helleiner 2014; Stuenkel 2016). Doing so leads us to also pay attention to complex contestation and interconnectedness. For instance, while subsidiarity may be used in Europe as a governance tool, it has been developed in Africa as a mechanism to manage institutional engagement in conflict among regional and global actors as well as among the AU and its recognized RECs. This is an important innovation even if the meaning and application of subsidiarity in this context is still under construction. In this instance, norm circulation, where norms come from multiple sources and contexts and are constantly subject to feedback, may be the most applicable theoretical model (Acharya 2013).

In addition to governance specializations, Africa and LAC have also developed innovative norms not seen at the international level prior to their use in Global South regions. ECOWAS, the subregional organization in West Africa, was the first IGO to deploy a peacekeeping mission to enforce peace in an internal conflict in the post–Cold War era. The ECOWAS Monitoring Group (ECOMOG) was deployed to Liberia without UNSC authorization in August 1990 ("Decision A/DEC.1/8/90 on the Ceasefire and Establishment of an ECOWAS Ceasefire Monitoring Group for Liberia (ECOWAS Peace Plan)" 1990). This was a precedent-setting mission that took place before the UNSC recognized the displacement of Kurds in Iraq as a threat to international peace and security in April 1991 ("Resolution 688 (1991) of 5 April 1991" 1991), much less before the authorization of a UN mission on Somalia justified on the basis of protecting civilians in a civil war ("Resolution 794 (1992): Adopted by the Security Council at Its 3145th Meeting, on 3 December 1992" 1992). The OAU and later the AU drew on ECOWAS actions when designing its more robust peace and security institutions, specifically citing the ECOWAS intervention as a model ("Report of the Secretary-General on the Establishment of a Mechanism for Conflict Prevention, Resolution, and Management" 1993, para. 133). Furthermore, several African statespersons helped to develop the ideas that went on to underpin the R2P doctrine, notably Francis Deng with his concept of sovereignty as responsibility. This reinterpretation of sovereignty contends that states are responsible for the safety of their citizens, and if a state is unable to fulfill this responsibility, then outside actors can interfere to protect civilians from atrocities. It reframes sovereignty as conferring responsibility instead of shielding a state from scrutiny of internal violence (Deng 1995; Deng et al. 1996). And yet, when developing the R2P doctrine, the International Commission on State Sovereignty and Intervention (ICISS) cites the North Atlantic Treaty Organization's unauthorized intervention in Kosovo as the primary impetus for an international norm on humanitarian intervention ("The Responsibility to Protect" 2001, VII). The ICISS report was released in December 2001, whereas the AU Constitutive Act that includes Article 4(h) outlining the use of humanitarian intervention was signed in July 2000 and ratified by May 2001.

Innovations from Latin America have also been marginalized in discussions about the development of global governance standards. Sikkink highlights the agency of Latin America and argues that "another way to talk about these processes of norm diffusion is to think of norm entrepreneurs in and from the Global South" (Sikkink 2015, 208). In particular, she demonstrates how the American Declaration of the Rights and Duties of Man preceded the UDHR when it was first approved in April 1948. This was eight months prior to the General Assembly adopting the UDHR in December 1948 (Sikkink 2015, 212). More importantly, Sikkink shows how Latin American delegates made important contributions during the drafting of the UDHR, particularly around provisions for economic and social rights (Sikkink 2015, 213–14).

More recently, the Inter-American Court has made key contributions to the development of indigenous rights. Several areas of relevant law at the global level are underspecified, including entitlement to land, the right to land or restitution for past dispossession, the use and ownership of subsurface resources within traditional lands, and the right of "free, prior, and informed consent" concerning decisions impacting indigenous communities (Tramontana 2010, 243–47). It is in precisely these areas where the Inter-American Court has deepened and clarified indigenous rights. On the issue of dispossession, the 2005 *Yakye Axa Indigenous Community* v. *Paraguay* case determined that it may be necessary to subordinate private property rights to preserve the cultural identities of indigenous groups. In cases where the states cannot return traditional lands, the Court held that states must provide comparable lands in consultation with the indigenous group and with their consent. If this cannot be done, then the people should be awarded compensation in an amount that takes into account not only the worth of the land but also the meaning of it to the indigenous community (Tramontana 2010, 254–55). Inter-American jurisprudence has also developed guidelines for the application of the concepts of consultation and consent, mandating a standard of effective participation and determining benchmarks for what this means in practice (Pentassuglia 2011, 178).

In their volume on governance transfer to regional institutions, Börzel and van Hüllen (2015) argue that regions are neither "passive recipients of a global script" nor "cultural containers whose particularities move them beyond comparison" (Börzel and van Hüllen 2015, 10). We agree with this assessment, but rather than understanding the development of regionalized governance as a process through which ROs "adapt and adopt global standards" (Börzel and van Hüllen 2015, 10), we are struck by the contributions of ROs to global norms and by the importance of internal drivers of regional specialization. We therefore find Acharya's concepts of norm circulation (2013) and/or idea-shift (2016a) more useful for our purposes than his concept of localization.

Acharya's concept of "idea-shifters" also emphasizes the potential for Global South agency. Here, he refers to "non-Western thinkers and practitioners" who have innovated "new concepts and approaches that have radically altered the way we think about development, security and ecology, among other areas" (Acharya 2016a, 1156). For example, while the Nuremburg Tribunal set an important precedent in the development of individual criminal responsibility for major atrocity crimes, LAC states were instrumental in the development of legal and political norms restricting the use of blanket amnesties, as discussed in Section 3. Transitional justice norms pioneered by post-transitional Latin America and the Caribbean constitute a major advance in the development in this accountability model. Similarly, while ideas about humanitarian intervention predate the end of the Cold War, ECOWAS arguably acted as a norm entrepreneur in its deployment of ECOMOG in Liberia.

4.2 Explaining Regional Differentiation

Peace and security governance is highly regionalized in Africa (compared to other Global South regions), while human rights accountability governance is highly regionalized in LAC (compared to other Global South regions). What accounts for this important variation? Our findings indicate that regions develop specializations, so diffusion of international norms is an inadequate explanation for the development of regional institutions and varying levels of governance regionalization. Instead, we emphasize the importance of the internal factors to the region that drive regionalization both in terms of the norms that regions create and the areas of governance they focus on. Our explanatory framework builds on the scholarship cited in Section 4.1 as well as our own work (particularly Coe 2019 and Nash 2021).

Our intention is not to present parsimonious theory but rather to draw on key insights from the comparative regionalism literature (and comparative politics/ international relations more generally) to make sense of regional governance specializations. We argue that a satisfactory explanation of the variation observed in Sections 2 and 3 requires attention to *regional* variation in material conditions and distribution of power; the dynamic history of ideas and institutions; relations with extraregional actors; and other unique regional experiences.

The African continent became a global leader in regional peace operations and peace process engagement to address conflicts in its own sphere in the post– Cold War era. Material conditions constitute a partial explanation, since there have been more post–Cold War intrastate conflicts to manage in Africa than in Latin America. The average "Civil Violence Magnitude and Impact" score for African countries was almost twice that of Latin American countries in the

1990s.[24] Distribution of (material) power also helps explain variation between the AU and the OAS in peace and security governance. Specifically, the membership of the global superpower – the United States – in the OAS has arguably strongly dissuaded the Latin American and Caribbean states from supporting formal regional mechanisms for military intervention.

However, we need more than this to understand broader variation across the Global South. Like Africa, Southeast Asia experienced a much higher rate of civil violence during the post–Cold War period than did Latin America,[25] but ASEAN stands out among Global South ROs for its aversion to conflict management activities that might be interpreted as interference. Furthermore, ASEAN does not boast a global superpower as a member, so we need to look beyond material factors for a more satisfactory explanation.

The "new institutionalisms" – including the discursive and historical varieties – help fill in some gaps. Discursive institutionalism pays attention, "not only the substantive content of ideas but also the interactive processes by which ideas are conveyed" (Schmidt 2008, 305). Any well-rounded explanation of the development of African regionalism needs to engage with the history of Pan-Africanism, a powerful macronational discourse that predates formal African regionalism by many decades and developed over time into a "Foucauldian 'regime of truth'" (Møller 2009, 57). Mumford (2021) argues that African international actors today are "locked in a Pan-African rhetorical trap," which she defines as "a normative environment in which certain outcomes become irresistible for a variety of actors because they accord unambiguously with the norms of the African community" (Mumford 2021). Importantly for our purposes, the history of Pan-Africanism reveals that this discourse has not been uncontested or static. In the lead-up to the creation of the OAU in 1963, two versions of Pan-Africanism competed with one another: a more conservative sovereignty-protective version and a radical sovereignty-challenging version (associated with the "United States of Africa" proposal). In the 1960s and 1970s, proponents of a more interventionist OAU drew upon the latter strain of Pan-Africanism to argue that the norm of noninterference ought not prevent the African community from formally sanctioning African leaders who came to power via force or committed atrocities against their people. Throughout the late 1970s, Tanzanian President Nyerere made this argument

---

[24] Based on the CIVTOT variable in the Center for Systemic Peace "Major Episodes of Political Violence (MEPV) AND Conflict Regions" dataset (July 25, 2019). Access codebook at www .systemicpeace.org/inscr/MEPVcodebook2018.pdf.

[25] Based on the CIVTOT variable in the Center for Systemic Peace "Major Episodes of Political Violence (MEPV) AND Conflict Regions" dataset (July 25, 2019). Access codebook at www .systemicpeace.org/inscr/MEPVcodebook2018.pdf.

in relation to Uganda's Idi Amin (Wheeler 2000, chap. 4). This contestation of noninterference in the name of Pan-Africanism served to erode strict sovereignty norms during the latter Cold War period (Coe 2019). Another way to conceptualize this process is that contradictions in the OAU's security culture predisposed this organization to be receptive to R2P later on (Williams 2007), although we would argue that this is not primarily a localization story.

There is a broad literature on the more immediate factors that contributed to African ROs adopting more interventionist peace and security policies in the 1990s and into the 2000s. As our recent work shows, we find the most convincing explanations to be those taking African agency seriously. Nash argues that evolving ideas and interests led to this change. Specifically, she traces changing conceptions of Pan-Africanism, new ideas around human security and sovereignty as responsibility, and the emergence of interests focused more on development and stability (following the end of white-minority regimes and a string of destabilizing conflicts). These evolving interests and ideas reframed African experiences with conflict during the Cold War period, prompting a shift in norms and institutions. Once this shift was underway, the conflicts and humanitarian catastrophes Africa experienced in the 1990s – along with UN failures on the continent – further pushed the AU to develop its peace and security capacity (Nash 2021). At this point, the influence of powerful African states and leaders helps explain the formal transition from the OAU to the AU, as Tieku has documented (Tieku 2004). In a similar vein, Coe views the end of the Cold War as a critical juncture and argues that both material and ideational developments in the 1980s (at the regional and global levels) conditioned the OAU's response to this juncture. First, Africa was worst hit by the severe economic crisis affecting much of the Global South during the 1980s. Second, international policy discourses developing both at the Economic Commission for Africa and within UN agencies emphasized the interconnectedness of security and economic development (development–security nexus). Finally, the end of superpower clientelism and the rise of "Afropessimism" contributed to the real and perceived marginalization of the continent by extraregional political and economic actors (Coe 2019). This combination of factors prompted some African regional bureaucrats and heads of state to campaign in the early 1990s for the development of formal regional mechanisms to manage civil conflict in order to create the conditions for development, manage Africa's image in the world, attract investors, and fulfill the promise of Pan-Africanism. The exact pathways of the transition in peace and security ideas, policies, and institutions in African ROs will continue to be scrutinized. Our findings are valuable in this ongoing discussion because they support the idea that diffusion from the global to the regional was not the determining factor. While we can see that extraregional developments (and actors) shaped regional institutional evolution in Africa, diffusion (or localization) is not the primary mechanism. The regionalization of human rights governance in LAC has also been driven primarily by internal events and processes. This region is increasingly recognized for its historical and contemporary role as a norm leader and innovator in the governance domains of both democracy and human rights (Santa-Cruz 2005; Sikkink 2015). In order to understand this specialization, a good starting place is the history of ideas in the region, as strong *legalist* and *liberal* (i.e. Enlightenment) discursive traditions date back to regional independence movements and the concomitant emergence of Pan-Americanism in the early nineteenth century (Kacowicz 2005; Obregón 2006, 2009). These traditions fed into Pan-Americanists' early concern with the protection of human rights, which has "long been an important theme in the region, having been discussed in successive Inter-American Conferences since the 1920s" (Serrano 2016, 431).

At the founding conference of the UN in 1945, Latin American states made up twenty of the fifty states present and thus comprised an important voting bloc. Latin American diplomats and NGOs lobbied the conference on the importance of including human rights in the UN Charter. Their success is evident by references to human rights throughout the Charter, and notably by the identification of human rights promotion as one of the purposes of the new organization (Sikkink 2015, 210). Sikkink argues that:

> The inclusion of human rights language in the Charter of the UN was a critical juncture that channeled the history of post-war global governance in the direction of setting international norms and law about the international promotion of human rights. This language was not of the Great Powers, and was finally adopted by the Great Powers only in response to pressures from smaller states and civil society. (Sikkink 2015, 211)

By 1948, the fledgling OAS had promulgated the first international declaration on human rights, which was adopted eight months prior to the UDHR. There was a strong emphasis on the inclusion of economic and social rights in the American Declaration that then influenced the UDHR. Latin American delegations pushed for a right to justice, and this right is reflected in Article 8 of the UDHR (Sikkink 2015, 213–14). The right to justice would also help to underpin some of the later innovations that emerged out of the IAHRS.

Historical institutionalism provides useful tools, like the concept of path dependency, for making sense of the development and persistence of Inter-American human rights institutions through the ebb and flow of democracy in the post–World War II period. Moments of higher democratic density[26] created openings for institutional development, and resultant institutions continued to operate – and take on "a life of their own" – during the height of military dictatorship and OAS irrelevance in the 1970s. A series of OAS decisions in the late 1950s and 1960s set the Inter-American system on a path that would result in the creation of the Inter-American Court by the late 1970s. The statute of the Inter-American Commission was approved in 1960 and its mandate broadened in 1965. Four years later, the ACHR (a legally binding document) gained approval. According to Mónica Serrano, "Through the 1960s the [regional human rights system] evolved surreptitiously, at times driven by decisions taken by regional governments, but most often by the country investigations and country reports issued by the Commission ... [which] positioned this organization as a 'guardian and critic' of regional human rights trends in the hemisphere" (Serrano 2016, 433). Importantly, the Inter-American Commission is an autonomous organ of the OAS, and its members serve in their personal capacity.

The investigation and reporting activities of the Commission became even more impactful in the late 1970s, when this body "began in earnest to test the limits of its authority – descending on countries, probing their viscera, and returning with graphic accounts of the stench" (Farer 1997, 510). It was not acting alone but rather as part of a network of human rights-oriented IGOs and NGOs that emerged in this decade and engaged in a variety of naming and shaming tactics to put pressure on repressive governments (Horwitz 2010, 45). In this way, regional discourses and institutions contributed to, participated in, and interacted with international and transnational movements rather than localizing European norms or a global script. External relations matter here, but they are not primary drivers of the IAHRS. By 1978, the ACHR entered into force and the Inter-American Court was created. While it is fair to say that Europe pioneered the idea of dividing a regional human rights system into a commission and court, a diffusion-based explanation for the strength of the Inter-American system is severely lacking, given the rich history of ideas and institutions summarized here.

Historical institutionalism's emphasis on timing and sequences is crucial for understanding the development of the Inter-American Court's jurisprudence, especially its attention to the domestic amnesty problem. To oversimplify, military dictators perpetrated atrocity crimes in the 1970s, widespread democ-ratization took place in the 1980s, and then the Cold War came to an end (contributing to the revitalization of multilateralism generally, including via

---

[26] Pevehouse (2005) coined this term.

ROs). The new LAC democracies that emerged from the 1980s found them-selves with legacies of repression to address and a renewed commitment to hemispheric regionalism. This confluence of factors carried important implica-tions for the Inter-American system. Specifically, a number of newly democratic states accepted the Court's jurisdiction and/or invited the Commission to carry out country visits for the first time, and the Commission saw a rise in petitions "seeking redress for past violations under authoritarian rule" (Goldman 2009, 875). The Commission responded by strengthening the petition system and referring a greater number of cases to the Court (Goldman 2009, 880). In the 1990s and beyond, some of the most innovative approaches by the Inter-American Court have been related to amnesty jurisprudence (Binder 2012, 297). Through a series of cases, the Court established that amnesty laws for perpetrators of particular human rights abuses violated the rights of victims to be heard and to judicial recourse (Binder 2012, 303).

4.3 Conclusions on Governance Regionalization: Extensions and Implications

4.3.1 Variation in Governance Regionalization

Governance is increasingly regionalized, but this regionalization varies across regions and issue areas. Specifically, this Element demonstrates that peace and security governance – both in terms of authority and ownership – is considerably more regionalized in Africa than in LAC. The APSA stands out among today's international regimes for the intrusive mandates of its constituent ROs, including its provision allowing for humanitarian intervention. It also stands out for the willing-ness of African ROs to deploy troops to ongoing conflict situations and for their relatively heavy involvement in peace processes. Although the UN maintains formal primacy and has purse-string power, these mechanisms to assert authority are subject to persistent negotiation by the AU. As African ROs have increasingly assumed ownership over peace missions and peace processes, they have translated this ownership into greater authority – although authority arguably continues to lag behind ownership in this case. The AU has also parlayed its increasing role and authority in peace and security issues to renegotiate the interpretation of key aspects of the UN Charter and the role of ROs in global peace and security.

Meanwhile, human rights governance is highly regionalized in Latin America and the Caribbean relative to other Global South regions. The Inter-American Commission assumes ownership of a much larger share of human rights governance labor through their quasi-judicial decisions on complaints – delivering decisions on roughly six to seven times as many complaints as institutions in the UNHRS. We argue that this is in part due to the greater authority of the regional body with respect to its jurisdiction. When it comes to judicial mechanisms, more LAC states are party to the Rome Statute and submit to the jurisdiction of the ICC than to the regional human rights court. However, the Inter-American Court has jurisdiction over a much wider set of rights, and it has enhanced its authority through intrusiveness, embeddedness, and innovative legal doctrines, including conventionality control. It has in turn asserted its authority to develop key areas of law, notably laws pertaining to amnesties and indigenous rights. Too often regions in the Global South are seen as the recipients of international law and not the sites of international law (Gathii 2020), but this is clearly not the case of the Inter-American system. Finally, the Inter-American Court is much more active in the Americas than is the ICC.

This Element has demonstrated regional specializations in two issue areas across two regions, but we do not think this is the end of the story. As our next brief example in Southeast Asia will show, regional governance specializations are continuing to emerge.

4.3.2 Extending the Analysis

Sections 2 and 3 highlight cases of highly regionalized governance in two regions with relatively strong ROs (in terms of authority vis-à-vis member states), but this phenomenon is not limited to cases of strong regionalism. ASEAN is a ten-member grouping in Southeast Asia that stands out in the Global South for its relatively steadfast commitment to sovereignty norms. The so-called ASEAN Way emphasizes "quiet" diplomacy, noninterference in domestic affairs, and consensus decision-making. ASEAN is less legalistic and more deferential to its member states than are the other ROs under study here. Because of this, it does not exercise authority vis-à-vis state governments to the same degree as other ROs, and it does not have strong conflict management or human rights institutions. ASEAN does, however, challenge UN primacy, particularly in the field of humanitarian assistance and disaster response (HADR). It also increasingly performs disaster response tasks (expanding ownership), via the ASEAN Coordinating Centre for Humanitarian Assistance on Disaster Management (AHA Centre). Compared to other issue areas, HADR governance is becoming highly regionalized here.

In the aftermath of the 2004 Indian Ocean earthquake and tsunami, ASEAN adopted the 2005 ASEAN Agreement on Disaster Management and Emergency Response ("ASEAN Agreement on Disaster Management and Emergency Response. Vientiane, 26 July 2005" 2005), followed six years later by the establishment of the ASEAN AHA Centre ("Agreement on the Establishment of the ASEAN Co-Ordinating Centre for Humanitarian Assistance on Disaster Management" 2011). The importance of the 2004 tsunami to this regional institutional development is not restricted to the event's material destructiveness. The disaster also brought about the so-called second tsunami, an "uncontrolled influx of Western aid agencies" which "drove home the realization that a regional mechanism may not just be a way of shoring up the widely diverging capacities of ASEAN member states, but also of mediating between their interests and those of extra-regional actors" (Spandler 2020a, 19–20).

The UN Office for the Coordination of Humanitarian Affairs (OCHA) has traditionally been central to the humanitarian system within which these extra-regional aid workers operate. However, the AHA Centre, established in 2011, works directly with the National Disaster Management Organizations, enhancing their capacity to respond to disasters. The Centre also crucially provides a coordination and informational management role vis-à-vis external actors and organizations. In this way, the regional body usurps to some degree the established leadership role of the UN OCHA and other UN agencies. It decenters the UN system and challenges its ownership of HADR in Southeast Asia, which in turn adds to its authority vis-à-vis global actors. It does not, however, assert authority against ASEAN member states or challenge their sovereignty. Rather, it defers to member state preferences and it enhances the ability of ASEAN governments to gatekeep extraregional actors in the aftermath of disaster. It enables member states to control the degree to which they will accept the intrusive aid and presence of outsiders (Coe and Spandler 2022).

By moving into this "hub" position, the AHA Centre has shifted the global–regional distribution of authority in the HADR policy domain. It has also increasingly taken on the labor of HADR governance with a broad mandate (Suzuki 2021, 408), augmenting regional ownership in three main categories of activity: disaster monitoring, preparedness and response, and capacity building ("What We Do" n.d.). This brief example of a recent emergence of a regional specialization highlights the diversity of regional strengths across issue areas and the need for continuing research on how regions have and are continuing to shape regional and global governance.

4.3.3 Implications for Global Governance and Global Order

Governance regionalization has already shaped global institutions and will continue to do so. The nature of this impact depends in part on the nature of UN–RO relations in a case of highly regionalized governance. These relations vary both in terms of interaction density and interaction type.[27] In the case of African security governance, we find highly dense global–regional interactions, and these interactions are sometimes cooperative and sometimes conflictual. In

---

[27] For a related typology, see Kacowicz's (2018) taxonomy of regional–global governance "links".

LAC human rights governance, by contrast, we instead find a global–regional nexus characterized by few interactions (low density). That is, the Inter-American system largely works in parallel (coexists) with the UN system with little cooperation or conflict. The case of Southeast Asian HADR governance looks more like the African security case.

The dense interactions we see in the African security regime have created new patterns of cooperation, as African ROs often act as first responders with the UN stepping in to support or implement longer-term missions. The RO's push for more autonomy and recognition in the peace and security issue area has also begun transforming understandings of UN primacy. In LAC, the Inter-American system has not entered into competition with the UN system, but the robust Inter-American jurisprudence on amnesty laws and subsequent domestic prosecutions may have produced a substitution effect, resulting in less engagement by international courts in the region. Furthermore, the Inter-American Court's rulings on justice rights and indigenous rights have the potential to advance the further legalization of these rights at the global level. In both instances, there is interplay between ownership and authority in the transformation of governance practices across levels of the international system. In many issues areas there are implicit if not explicit notions of hierarchy that often go unexplored when analyzing nested institutions. Exploring the relationship between ownership and authority is one way to analyze how authority is contested and ultimately how it might be reconstructed.

Global order has long been influenced by an array of actors, including Global South actors (Coleman and Tieku 2018; Helleiner 2014; Sikkink 2015). There is nonetheless a dearth of scholarship on these contributions. Beyond historic contributions, Global South actors are only going to grow more prominent in an evolving global order that includes an expanded global marketplace of ideas and actors beyond major powers shaping powerful discourses (Carothers and Samet-Marram 2015). The evolution of the global order and the number of actors that will insist on a stake in it is likely to accelerate in the wake of declining trust in major powers as well as institutions, such as the World Health Organization, in the wake of the COVID-19 pandemic. This Element has explored the governance specializations of two regions, and while the impact of these regional specializations is not the focus of this Element, it is clear that both Africa and LAC are leaving their mark and potentially diffusing norms to other regions. Further scholarship is needed on the regionalized dimensions of global governance.

Abbreviations

ACHR	American Convention on Human Rights
ACtHPR	African Court on Human and People's Rights
AfHRS	African human rights system
AHA Centre	ASEAN Coordinating Centre for Humanitarian Assistance on Disaster Management
AMIS	African Mission in Sudan
APSA	African Peace and Security Architecture
ASEAN	Association of Southeast Asian Nations
AU	African Union
CEDAW	Convention on the Elimination of All Forms of Discrimination Against Women
ECOWAS	Economic Community of West African States
ECOMOG	ECOWAS Monitoring Group
EU	European Union
HADR	Humanitarian assistance and disaster response
IAHRS	Inter-American human rights system
ICC	International Criminal Court
ICCPR	International Covenant on Civil and Political Rights
ICISS	International Commission on Intervention and State Sovereignty
IGOs	Intergovernmental organizations
IOR	Interorganizational relations
JEM	Justice and Equality Movement
LAC	Latin America and the Caribbean
NGOs	Nongovernmental organizations
OAU	Organization of African Unity
OCHA	UN Office for the Coordination of Humanitarian Affairs
PSC	(AU) Peace and Security Council
RECs	Regional Economic Communities
ROs	Regional organizations
SLM	Sudan Liberation Movement
UDHR	Universal Declaration of Human Rights
UN	United Nations
UNHRS	United Nations human rights system
UNSC	United National Security Council

References

Abebe, Zekarias Beshah. 2017. "The African Court with a Criminal Jurisdiction and the ICC: A Case for Overlapping Jurisdiction?" *African Journal on International and Comparative Law* 23 (5): 418–29.

"About UNAMID." n.d. United Nations. Accessed October 28, 2020. https://unamid.unmissions.org/about-unamid-0.

Acharya, Amitav. 2004. "How Ideas Spread: Whose Norms Matter? Norm Localization and Institutional Change in Asian Regionalism." *International Organization* 58 (Spring): 239–75.

2013. "The R2P and Norm Diffusion: Towards a Framework of Norm Circulation." *Global Responsibility to Protect* 5: 466–79.

2016a. "Idea-Shift: How Ideas from the Rest Are Reshaping Global Order." *Third World Quarterly* 37 (7): 1156–70.

2016b. "Regionalism Beyond EU-Centrism." In *The Oxford Handbook of Comparative Regionalism*, edited by Tanja A. Börzel and Thomas Risse, 109–30. Oxford University Press.

"African (Banjul) Charter on Human and People's Rights." 1986. Organization of African Unity. https://au.int/en/treaties/african-charter-human-and-peoples-rights.

African Union Commission. 2015. *African Union Handbook 2015*. African Union Commission and New Zealand Ministry of Foreign Affairs.

"Agreement on the Establishment of the ASEAN Co-Ordinating Centre for Humanitarian Assistance on Disaster Management." 2011. ASEAN. https://ahacentre.org/publication/the-agreement-of-the-establishment-of-the-aha-centre/.

"Agreement with the Sudanese Parties on the Modalities for the Establishment of the Ceasefire Commission and the Deployment of Observers in the Darfur." 2004. www.peaceagreements.org/view/92.

Akinkugbe, Olabisi D. 2020. "Towards an Analysis of the Mega-Politics Jurisprudence of the ECOWAS Community Court of Justice." In *The Performance of Africa's International Courts: Using International Litigation for Political, Legal, and Social Change*, edited by James Thuo Gathii, 149–177. Oxford University Press.

Alter, Karen J., Laurence R. Helfer, and Jacqueline R. McAllister. 2013. "A New International Human Rights Court for West Africa: The ECOWAS Community Court of Justice." *American Journal of International Law* 107: 737–79.

Alter, Karen J., and Sophie Meunier. 2009. "The Politics of International Regime Complexity." *Perspectives on Politics* 7 (1): 13–24.

Alter, Karen J., and Kal Raustiala. 2018. "The Rise of International Regime Complexity." *Annual Review of Law and Social Science* 14: 329–49.

"American Convention on Human Rights." (1969) 1978. Organization of American States. www.cidh.oas.org/basicos/english/basic3.american% 20convention.htm.

"American Declaration of the Rights and Duties of Man." 1948. Organization of American States. www.oas.org/en/iachr/mandate/Basics/declaration.asp.

Antkowiak, Thomas M. 2008. "Remedial Approaches to Human Rights Violations: The Inter-American Court of Human Rights and Beyond." *Columbia Journal of Transnational Law* 46 (2): 351–419.

Aris, Stephen, and Aglaya Snetkov. 2018. "Cooperating and Competing: Relations between Multilateral Organizations in International Security." In *Inter-Organizational Relations in International Security: Cooperation and Competition*, edited by Stephen Aris, Aglaya Snetkov, and Andreas Wenger, E-reader. Taylor & Francis.

"ASEAN Agreement on Disaster Management and Emergency Response. Vientiane, 26 July 2005." 2005. ASEAN. https://asean.org/speechandstate ment/asean-agreement-on-disaster-management-and-emergency-response-vientiane-26-july-2005/.

"Assembly of States Parties to the Rome Statute." n.d. International Criminal Court. Accessed June 9, 2022. https://asp.icc-cpi.int/states-parties.

Baranyi, Stephen. 1995. "Peace Missions and Subsidiarity in the Americas: Conflict Management in the Western Hemisphere." *International Journal* 50 (2): 343–69.

Barber, N. W. 2005. "The Limited Modesty of Subsidiarity." *European Law Journal* 11 (3): 308–25.

Barrios Altos v. Peru. 2001. Inter-American Court of Human Rights.

"Basic Information." n.d. African Court on Human and Peoples' Rights. Accessed May 31, 2022. www.african-court.org/wpafc/basic-information/.

Bell, Christine. 2006. "Peace Agreements: Their Nature and Legal Status." *The American Journal of International Law* 100: 373–412.

Bell, Christine, Sanja Badanjak, Robert Forster, Astrid Jamar, Jan Pospisil, Laura Wise, 2017. *PA-X Codebook, Version 1.* Political Settlements Research Programme, University of Edinburgh. www.peaceagreements .org.

Bellamy, Alex J., and Paul D. Williams. 2011. "The New Politics of Protection? Côte D'Ivoire, Libya and the Responsibility to Protect." *International Affairs* 87 (4): 825–50.

Binder, Christina. 2012. "The Prohibition of Amnesties by the Inter-American Court of Human Rights." In *International Judicial Lawmaking*, edited by Armin von Bogdandy and Ingo Venzke, 295–328. Springer Berlin Heidelberg.

Blavoukos, Spyros, and Dimitris Bourantonis. 2017. "Nested Institutions." In *Palgrave Handbook of Inter-Organizational Relations in World Politics*, edited by Rafael Biermann and Joachim A. Koops, 303–17. Palgrave Macmillan.

2018. "Inter-Organizational Relations in a Nested Environment." In *Inter-Organizational Relations in International Security: Cooperation and Competition*, edited by Stephen Aris, Aglaya Snetkov, and Andreas Wenger, E-reader. Taylor & Francis.

Boehme, Franziska. 2017. "'We Chose Africa': South Africa and the Regional Politics of Cooperation with the International Criminal Court." *International Journal of Transitional Justice* 11 (1): 50–70.

Börzel, Tanja A., and Vera van Hüllen, eds. 2015. *Governance Transfer by Regional Organizations: Patching Together a Global Script*. Palgrave Macmillan.

Börzel, Tanja A., and Thomas Risse. 2016. "Introduction: Framework of the Handbook and Conceptual Clarifications." In *The Oxford Handbook of Comparative Regionalism*, edited by Tanja A. Börzel and Thomas Risse, 3–15. Oxford University Press.

2019. "Grand Theories of Integration and the Challenges of Comparative Regionalism." *Journal of European Public Policy* 26 (8): 1231–52. https://doi.org/10.1080/13501763.2019.1622589.

2021. "Regional and Global MLG Between and Beyond States," In *A Research Agenda for Multi-level Governance*, edited by Arthur Benz, Jörg Broschek and Markus Lederer, Edward Elgar: 117–134.

Brosig, Malte. 2015. *Cooperative Peacekeeping in Africa: Exploring Regime Complexity*. Routledge.

2020. "Whither a Theory of Inter-Organisational Relations: A Burgeon Field of Research between Conceptual Innovation and Fragmentation." *Journal of Intervention and Statebuilding* 14 (2): 171–86.

Carothers, Thomas, and Oren Samet-Marram. 2015. "The New Global Marketplace of Political Change." *Carnegie Endowment for International Peace*. https://carnegieendowment.org/2015/04/20/new-glo bal-marketplace-of-political-change-pub-59808.

"Cases." n.d. International Criminal Court. Accessed July 24, 2022. www.icc-cpi.int/cases.

"Charter of the Organization of American States." 1951. Organization of American States. www.oas.org/en/sla/dil/inter_american_treaties_A-41_charter_OAS.asp.

"Charter of the United Nations." 1945. United Nations. www.un.org/en/charter-united-nations/.

Cimiotta, Emanuele. 2017. "'Triangular' Relationships between the United Nations and Regional and Sub-Regional Organizations in Maintaining Peace." *International Organizations Law Review* 14: 321–45.

Coe, Brooke. 2015. "Sovereignty Regimes and the Norm of Noninterference in the Global South: Regional and Temporal Variation." *Global Governance* 21: 275–98.

2019. *Sovereignty in the South: Intrusive Regionalism in Africa, Latin America, and Southeast Asia.* Cambridge University Press.

Coe, Brooke, and Kathryn Nash. 2020. "Peace Process Protagonism: The Role of Regional Organisations in Africa in Conflict Management." *Global Change, Peace & Security* 32 (2): 157–77.

Coe, Brooke, and Kilian Spandler. 2022. "Beyond Effectiveness: The Political Functions of ASEAN's Disaster Governance." *Global Governance,* 28 (3) 355–81.

Coleman, Katharina P., and Thomas Kwasi Tieku. 2018. "African Actors in International Security: Four Pathways to Influence." In *African Actors in International Security: Shaping Contemporary Norms,* edited by Katharina P. Coleman and Thomas Kwasi Tieku, 1–20. Lynne Rienner.

"Communications Procedure." n.d. African Commission on Human and Peoples' Rights. Accessed May 31, 2022. www.achpr.org/communications procedure.

"Consolidated Version of the Treaty on European Union." 1993. European Union. https://eur-lex.europa.eu/resource.html?uri=cellar:2bf140bf-a3f8-4ab2-b506-fd71826e6da6.0023.02/DOC_1&format=PDF.

"Constitutive Act of the African Union." 2001. African Union. https://au.int/en/treaties/constitutive-act-african-union.

Craig, Paul. 2012. "Subsidiarity: A Political and Legal Analysis." *Journal of Common Market Studies* 50 (S1): 72–87.

Daly, Gerald, and Micha Wiebusch. 2018. "The African Court on Human and Peoples' Rights: Mapping Resistance against a Young Court." *International Journal of Law in Context* 14 (2): 294–313.

Darkwa, Linda. 2018. "Humanitarian Intervention." In *African Actors in International Security: Shaping Contemporary Norms,* edited by Thomas Kwasi Tieku and Katharina P. Coleman, 21–38. Lynne Rienner.

de Coning, Cedric, Linnéa Gelot, and John Karlsrud. 2016. "Towards an African Model of Peace Operations." In *The Future of African Peace Operations: From the Janjaweed to Boko Haram,* edited by de Coning, Cedric, Linnea Gelot, and John Karlsrud, 1–19. Zed Books.

"Decision A/DEC.1/8/90 on the Ceasefire and Establishment of an ECOWAS Ceasefire Monitoring Group for Liberia (ECOWAS Peace Plan)." 1990. Economic Community of West African States. www.peaceagreements .org/view/1305.

"Decisions of First Mid-Year Coordination Meeting between the African Union, the Regional Economic Communities and the Regional Mechanisms." 2019. African Union. https://au.int/en/decisions/decisions-first-mid-year-coordin ation-meeting-between-au-recs-and-regional-mechanisms.

"Declaration on Security in the Americas." 2003. Organization of American States. www.oas.org/en/sms/docs/declaration%20security%20americas% 20rev%201%20-%2028%20oct%202003%20ce00339.pdf.

Deng, Francis. 1995. "Reconciling Sovereignty with Responsibility: A Basis for International Humanitarian Action." In *Africa in World Politics: Post Cold War Challenges*, 2nd ed., edited by John W. Harbeson and Donald Rothchild, 295–310. West View Press.

Deng, Francis, Sadikiel Kimaro, Terrence Lyons, Donald Rothchild, and I. William Zartman. 1996. *Sovereignty as Responsibility: Conflict Management in Africa*. Brookings Institute Press.

Dersso, Solomon. 2013. "The African Union." In *An Institutional Approach to the Responsibility to Protect*, edited by Gentian Zyberi, 220–46. Cambridge University Press.

Desmidt, Sophie. 2019. "Conflict Management and Prevention under the African Peace and Security Architecture (APSA) of the African Union." *African Journal of Management* 5 (1): 79–97.

Dominguez, Roberto. 2017. "Security Governance in Latin America." In *Power Dynamics and Regional Security*, edited by Marcial A. G. Suarez, Rafael Duarte Villa, and Brigitte Weiffen, 53–76. Palgrave Macmillan.

"ECOWAS Protocol Relating to the Mechanism for Conflict Prevention, Management, Resolution, Peace-Keeping, and Security." 1999. Economic Community of West African States. www.zif-berlin.org/filead min/uploads/analyse/dokumente/ECOWAS_Protocol_ConflictPrevention .pdf.

Engberg, Katarina. 2015. "Trends in Conflict Management: Multilateral Intervention and the Role of Regional Organizations." In *Regional Organizations and Peacemaking: Challengers to the UN?* edited by Peter Wallensteen and Anders Bjurner, 72–85. Routledge.

Engstrom, Par, and Peter Low. 2019. "Mobilising the Inter-American Human Rights System: Regional Litigation and Domestic Human Rights Impact in Latin America." In *The Inter-American Human Rights System: Impact Beyond Compliance*, edited by Par Engstrom, 23–58. Palgrave Macmillan.

Farer, Tom. 1997. "The Rise of the Inter-American Human Rights Regime: No Longer a Unicorn, Not Yet an Ox." *Human Rights Quarterly* 19 (3): 510–46.

Fioramonti, Lorenzo, and Frank Mattheis. 2016. "Is Africa Really Following Europe? An Integrated Framework for Comparative Regionalism." *Journal of Common Market Studies* 54 (3): 674–90.

Gathii, James Thuo. 2020. "Promise of International Law: A Third World View (Including a TWAIL Bibliography 1996–2019 as an Appendix)." *Proceedings of the ASIL Annual Meeting* 114: 165–87.

Gelot, Linnéa. 2015. "African Regional Organizations, Peace Operations, and the UN: Legitimacy & Disengagement." In *Regional Organizations and Peacemaking: Challengers to the UN?*, edited by Peter Wallensteen and Anders Bjurner. Routledge.

Goldman. Robert K. 2009. "History and Action: The Inter-American Human Rights System and the Role of the Inter-American Commission on Human Rights." *Human Rights Quarterly* 31(4):856–87. www.jstor.org/stable/40389979.

"Growth in United Nations Membership, 1945–Present." n.d. United Nations. Accessed March 12, 2021. www.un.org/en/about-us/growth-in-un-membership.

Hampson, Françoise, Claudia Martin, and Frans Viljoen. 2018. "Inaccessible Apexes: Comparing Access to Regional Human Rights Courts and Commissions in Europe, the Americas, and Africa," *International Journal of Constitutional Law 16*, no. 1: 163.

Helleiner, Eric. 2014. "Principles from the Periphery: The Neglected Southern Sources of Global Norms." *Global Governance* 20 (3): 359–60.

Herz, Mônica. 2011. *The Organization of American States: Global Governance Away from the Media*. Routledge.

Herz, Monica, Maira Siman, and Ana Clara Telles. 2017. "Regional Organizations, Conflict Resolution and Mediation in South America." In *Power Dynamics and Regional Security in Latin America*, edited by Marcial A. G. Suarez, Rafael Duarte Villa, and Brigitte Weiffen, 123–48. Palgrave Macmillan.

Hillebrecht, Courtney, Alexandra Huneeus, and Sandra Borda. 2018. "The Judicialization of Peace." *Harvard International Law Journal* 59 (2): 279–330.

Horwitz, Betty. 2010. *The Transformation of the Organization of American States: A Multilateral Framework for Regional Governance*. Anthem Press.

Huneeus, Alexandra. 2013. "International Criminal Law by Other Means: The Quasi-Criminal Jurisdiction of the Human Rights Courts." *American*

Journal of International Law 107 (1): 1–44. https://doi.org/10.5305/ amerjintelaw.107.1.0001.

2015. "Reforming the State from Afar: Structural Reform Litigation at the Human Rights Courts." *Yale Journal of International Law* 40 (1): 1–38.

2018. "Legitimacy and Jurisdictional Overlap: The ICC and the Inter-American Court in Colombia." In *Legitimacy and International Courts*, edited by Nienke Grossman, Harlan Grant Cohen, Andreas Follesdal, and Geir Ulfstein, 114–42. Cambridge University Press.

Huneeus, Alexandra, and Mikael Rask Madsen. 2018. "Between Universalism and Regional Law and Politics: A Comparative History of the American, European, and African Human Rights Systems." *International Journal of Constitutional Law* 16 (1): 136–60.

"Identical Letters Dated 21 August 2000 from the Secretary-General to the President of the General Assembly and the President of the Security Council: Report of the Panel on United Nations Peace Operations." 2000. UN General Assembly. www.refworld.org/docid/49997ac61a.html.

"Important Dates." n.d. African Commission on Human and Peoples' Rights. Accessed July 15, 2021. www.achpr.org/dates.

"Individual Communications." n.d. United Nations Office of the High Commissioner of Human Rights. Accessed July 24, 2022. www.ohchr .org/en/treaty-bodies/ccpr/individual-communications.

"Inter-American Commission on Human Rights: Statistics." n.d. Organization of American States. Accessed July 29, 2021. www.oas.org/en/iachr/multi media/statistics/statistics.html.

"Inter-American Human Rights System." n.d. International Justice Research Center. Accessed June 24, 2022. https://ijrcenter.org/regional/inter-ameri can-system/#Inter-American_Court_of_Human_Rights.

"International Civilian Support Mission in Haiti (MICAH)." n.d. United Nations Archives and Records Management Section. Accessed June 28, 2022. https://search.archives.un.org/international-civilian-support-mis sion-in-haiti-micah.

"International Courts." 2022. United States Department of Justice. www.just ice.gov/jmd/ls/international-courts.

"International Covenant on Civil and Political Rights." (1966) 1976. United Nations. www.ohchr.org/en/professionalinterest/pages/ccpr.aspx.

Jetschke, Anja. 2019. *The Military and Non-Military Interventions (MILINDA) Codebook.* University of Goettingen, http://lehrstuhlib.uni-goettingen.de/ milinda.html.

Kacowicz, Arie M. 2005. *The Impacts of Norms in International Society: The Latin American Experience, 1881–2001.* University of Notre Dame Press.

Kacowicz. Arie M. 2018. "Regional Governance and Global Governance: Links and Explanations." *Global Governance*, 24 (1): 61–79. www.jstor .org/stable/44861170.

Kirmse, Stefan B. 2014. "Sleepy Side Alleys, Dead Ends, and the Perpetuation of Eurocentrism." *European Journal of International Law* 25 (1): 307–11.

Knight, W. Andy. 1996. "Towards a Subsidiarity Model for Peacemaking and Preventive Diplomacy: Making Chapter VIII of the UN Charter Operational." *Third World Quarterly* 17 (1): 31–52.

Koops, Joachim A. 2017. "Inter-Organizationalism in International Relations: A Multilevel Framework of Analysis." In *Palgrave Handbook of Inter-Organizational Relations in World Politics*, edited by Joachim A. Koops and Rafael Biermann, 189–216. Palgrave Macmillan.

Lind, Gustaf. 2015. "Chapter VIII of the UN Charter: Its Revival and Significant Today." In *Regional Organizations and Peacemaking: Challengers to the UN?* edited by Peter Wallensteen and Anders Blumer, 28–38. Routledge.

Lotze, Walter. 2018. "Challenging the Primacy of the UN Security Council." In *African Actors in International Security: Shaping Contemporary Norms*, edited by Katharina P. Coleman and Thomas K. Tieku, 219–40. Lynne Rienner.

Lundgren, Magnus. 2016. "Conflict Management Capabilities of Peace-Brokering International Organizations, 1945–2010: A New Dataset." *Conflict Management and Peace Science* 33 (2): 198–223.

McEvoy, Joanne, 2017. "Inter-Organizational Coordination in Peacebuilding," In *Palgrave Handbook of Inter-Organizational Relations in World Politics*, edited by Joachim A. Koops and Rafael Biermann, 429–45. Palgrave Macmillan.

"Memorandum of Understanding on Cooperation in the Area of Peace and Security between the African Union, the Regional Economic Communities and the Coordinating Mechanisms of the Regional Standby Brigades of Eastern and Northern Africa." 2008. African Union. www .peaceau.org/uploads/mou-au-rec-eng.pdf.

Merry, Sally Engle. 2006. "Transnational Human Rights and Local Activism." *American Anthropologist* 108 (1): 38–51.

"Mission Description." n.d. European Union. Accessed October 28, 2020. https://eeas.europa.eu/archives/csdp/missions-and-operations/eu-support-amis-darfur/mission-description/index_en.htm.

Møller, Bjørn. 2009. "The African Union as Security Actor: African Solutions to African Problems?" Working Paper no. 57. *Regional and Global Axes of Conflict*. http://eprints.lse.ac.uk/28485/1/WP57.2Moller.AU.pdf.

Mumford, Densua. 2020. "Comparative Regionalism's Decolonial Turn: A Proposition." *E-International Relations*. www.e-ir.info/2020/10/03/comparative-regionalisms-decolonial-turn-a-proposition/.

2021. "How Regional Norms Shape Regional Organizations: The Pan-African Rhetorical Trap and the Empowerment of the ECOWAS Parliament." *African Affairs* 120 (478): 1–25.

Murithi, Tim. 2018. "Localizing Transitional Justice Norms." In *African Actors in International Security: Shaping Contemporary Norms*, edited by Katharina P. Coleman and Thomas K. Tieku, 153–72. Lynne Rienner.

Murray, Rachel. 2019. "The Human Rights Jurisdiction of the African Court of Justice and Human and Peoples' Rights." In *The African Court of Justice and Human and Peoples' Rights in Context: Development and Challenges*, edited by Charles C. Jalloh, Kamari M. Clarke, and Vincent O. Nmehielle, 965–88. Cambridge University Press.

Nash, Kathryn. 2021. *African Peace: Regional Norms from the Organizuuion of African Unity to the African Union*. Manchester University Press.

Nathan, Laurie. 2017. "How to Manage Interorganizational Disputes over Mediation in Africa." *Global Governance* 23: 151–62.

Ndiaye, Michelle. 2016. "The Relationship between the AU and the RECs/RMs in Relation to Peace and Security in Africa: Subsidiarity and Inevitable Common Destiny." In *The Future of African Peace Operations: From the Janjaweed to Boko Haram*, edited by Cedric de Coning, Linnéa Gelot, and John Karlsrud, 52–64. Zed Books.

Nel, Michelle. 2020. "From Peacekeeping to Stabilisation: Interorganisational Co-Operation, Challenges and the Law." *Journal of Intervention and Statebuilding* 14 (2): 237–52.

Nowak, Manfred. 2007. "The Need for a World Court of Human Rights." *Human Rights Law Review* 7: 251–59.

Obregón, Liliana. 2006. "Creole Consciousness and International Law in Nineteenth Century Latin America." In *International Law and Its Others*, edited by Anne Orford, 247–64. Cambridge University Press.

2009. "Latin American International Law." In *Routledge Handbook of International Law*, edited by David Armstrong, 154–64. Routledge.

2019. "Peripheral Histories of International Law." *Annual Review of Law and Social Science* 15 (1): 437–51.

O'Brien, David. 2000. "The Search for Subsidiarity: The UN, African Regional Organizations and Humanitarian Action." *International Peacekeeping* 7 (3): 57–83. https://doi.org/10.1080/13533310008413849.

Orsini, Amandine, Jean-Frederic Morin, and Oran Young. 2013. "Regime Complexes: A Buzz, a Boom, or a Boost for Global Governance." *Global Governance* 19: 27–39.

Orsini, Amandine, Philippe Le Prestre, Peter M Haas, Malte Brosig, Philipp Pattberg, Oscar Widerberg, Laura Gomez-Mera, Jean-Frédéric Morin, Neil E Harrison, Robert Geyer, David Chandler, et al. 2020. "Forum: Complex Systems and International Governance," *International Studies Review*, (22) 4: 1008–38. https://doi.org/10.1093/isr/viz005.

Pentassuglia, Gaetano. 2011. "Towards a Jurisprudential Articulation of Indigenous Land Rights." *The European Journal of International Law* 22 (1): 165–202.

Perez-Leon-Acevedo, Juan Pablo. 2020. "The Control of the Inter-American Court of Human Rights over Amnesty Laws and Other Exemption Measures: Legitimacy Assessment." *Leiden Journal of International Law* 33: 667–87.

Pevehouse, Jon, Timothy Nordstrom, and Kevin Warnke. 2004. "The COW-2 International Organizations Dataset Version 2.0." *Conflict Management and Peace Science* 21 (2): 101–19.

Pevehouse, Jon. 2005. *Democracy from Above: Regional Organisations and Democratization*. Cambridge University Press. www.cambridge.org/gb/academic/subjects/politics-international-relations/comparative-politics/democracy-above-regional-organizations-and-democratization?format=PB.

Pinto, Monica. 1999. "Fragmentation or Unification among International Institutions: Human Rights Tribunals." *New York University Journal of International Law and Politics* 31 (4): 833–42.

Polgreen, Lydia. 2008. " Court Rules Niger Failed by Allowing Girl's Slavery." *New York Times*. October 27. Accessed October 12, 2022. https://www.nytimes.com/2008/10/28/world/africa/28niger.html

"Population, Total – Latin American and Caribbean." n.d. World Bank. Accessed June 24, 2022. https://data.worldbank.org/indicator/SP.POP.TOTL?locations=ZJ.

"Population, Total – Sub-Saharan Africa." n.d. World Bank. Accessed June 24, 2022. https://data.worldbank.org/indicator/SP.POP.TOTL?locations=ZG.

Postel-Vinay, Karoline. 2020. "Regionality and Globality: Two Sides of the Same Narrative." In *The Multidimensionality of Regions in World Politics*, edited by Paul J. Kohlenberg and Nadine Godehardt, E-reader. Taylor & Francis.

Pratt, Tyler. 2018. "Deference and Hierarchy in International Regime Complexes." *International Organization* 72 (3): 561–90.

"Press Release: The Mission to Support the Peace Process in Colombia (MAPP/ OAS)." 2016. Organization of American States. www.oas.org/en/media_ center/press_release.asp?sCodigo=S-017/16.

"Protocol on Amendments to the Protocol on the Statute of the African Court of Justice and Human Rights." (2014) Not in force. https://au.int/en/treaties/ protocol-amendments-protocol-statute-african-court-justice-and-human-rights.

"Protocol Relating to the Establishment of the Peace and Security Council of the African Union." 2003. African Union. https://au.int/sites/default/files/treat ies/7781-treaty-0024_-_protocol_relating_to_the_establishment_of_the_ peace_and_security_council_of_the_african_union_e.pdf.

"Protocol to the African Charter on Human and Peoples' Rights on the Establishment of an African Court on Human and Peoples' Rights." (1998) 2004. African Union. https://au.int/en/treaties/protocol-african-charter-human-and-peoples-rights-establishment-african-court-human-and.

Rachovitsa, Adamantia. 2019. "On New 'Judicial Animals': The Curious Case of an African Court with Material Jurisdiction of a Global Scope." *Human Rights Law Review* 19: 255–89.

Raustiala, Kal, and David G. Victor. 2004. "The Regime Complex for Plant Genetic Resources." *International Organization* 58 (2): 277–309.

Reinold, Theresa. 2019. "The Promises and Perils of Subsidiarity in Global Governance: Evidence from Africa." *Third World Quarterly* 40 (11): 2092–107.

"Report of the Secretary-General on the Establishment of a Mechanism for Conflict Prevention, Resolution, and Management." 1993. Organization of African Unity. African Union Commission.

"Report of the Secretary-General on the Workshop on Regional Arrangements for the Promotion and Protection of Human Rights, 24 and 25 November 2008." 2009. United Nations. A/HRC/11/3. https://ap .ohchr.org/documents/dpage_e.aspx?si=A/HRC/11/3.

"Resolution 688 (1991) of 5 April 1991." 1991. United Nations. http://unscr .com/en/resolutions/688.

"Resolution 794 (1992): Adopted by the Security Council at Its 3145th Meeting, on 3 December 1992." 1992. United Nations. http://unscr.com/ en/resolutions/794.

Risse, Thomas. 2016. "The Diffusion of Regionalism." In *The Oxford Handbook of Comparative Regionalism*, edited by Tanja A. Börzel and Thomas Risse, 87–108. Oxford University Press.

Rodriguez, J. Luis. 2020. "Crafting Constraints: Latin American Support for Humanitarian-Intervention Norms." *Third World Quarterly* 43 (5): 1217–35. https://doi.org/10.1080/01436597.2022.2057944.

Roht-Arriaza, Naomi. 2019. "Transitional Justice in Latin America: Achievements and Limitations." Research Paper no. 309. *UC Hastings College of Law Legal Studies Research Paper Series*.

"Rome Statute of the International Criminal Court." 2002. International Criminal Court. www.icc-cpi.int/sites/default/files/RS-Eng.pdf.

Sandner, Philipp. 2020. "Africa's Court of Human Rights on the Brink of Collapse." *DW*. www.dw.com/en/africas-court-of-human-rights-on-the-brink-of-collapse/a-53776946.

Santa-Cruz, Arturo. 2005. "Constitutional Structures, Sovereignty, and the Emergence of Norms: The Case of International Election Monitoring." *International Organization* 59 (3): 663–93.

Schmidt, Vivien A. 2008. "Discursive Institutionalism: The Explanatory Power of Ideas and Discourse." *Annual Review of Political Science* 11: 303–26.

"Secretariat for Multidimensional Security." n.d. Organization of American States. Accessed September 4, 2018. www.oas.org/en/about/sms.asp.

"Securing Predictable and Sustainable Financing for Peace in Africa." 2016. African Union. www.peaceau.org/uploads/auhr-progress-report-final-020916-with-annexes.pdf.

Serrano, Mónica. 2016. "Latin America." In *The Oxford Handbook of the Responsibility to Protect*, edited by Alex J. Bellamy and Tim Dunne, 429–50. Oxford University Press.

Sikkink, Kathryn. 2011. *The Justice Cascade: How Human Rights Prosecutions Are Changing World Politics*. Norton.

2015. "Latin America's Protagonist Role in Human Rights." *International Journal on Human Rights* 12 (22): 207–18.

"South American Union of Nations Constitutive Treaty." 2011. South American Union of Nations. https://web.archive.org/web/20130807093918/http://unasursg.org/uploads/0c/c7/0cc721468628d65c3c510a577e54519d/Tratado-constitutivo-english-version.pdf.

Spandler, Kilian. 2020a. "Saving People or Saving Face? Four Narratives of Regional Humanitarian Order in Southeast Asia." *The Pacific Review*, 35: 172–201.

2020b. "UNAMID and the Legitimation of Global-Regional Peacekeeping Cooperation: Partnership and Friction in UN-AU Relations." *Journal of Intervention and Statebuilding* 14 (2): 187–203.

"Status List: Protocol on Amendments to the Protocol on the Statute of the African Court of Justice and Human Rights." 2019. African Union.

https://au.int/sites/default/files/treaties/36398-sl-PROTOCOL%20ON% 20AMENDMENTS%20TO%20THE%20PROTOCOL%20ON%20THE %20STATUTE%20OF%20THE%20AFRICAN%20COURT%20OF% 20JUSTICE%20AND%20HUMAN%20RIGHTS.pdf.

Stefanova, Boyka. 2006. "Regional Integration as a System for Conflict Resolution: The European Experience." *World Affairs* 169 (2): 81–93.

Stuenkel, Oliver. 2016. *Post-Western World: How Emerging Powers Are Remaking Global Order.* Polity Press.

Suzuki, Sanae. 2021. "Interfering via ASEAN? In the Case of Disaster Management." *Journal of Current Southeast Asian Affairs* 40 (3): 400–17. https://doi.org/10.1177/18681034211016865.

"The Common African Position on the Proposed Reform of the United Nations: The Ezulwini Consensus." 2005. African Union Executive Council. www .un.org/en/africa/osaa/pdf/au/cap_screform_2005.pdf.

"The Lusaka Manifesto on Southern Africa Proclaimed by the Fifth Summit Conference of East and Central African States." 1969. Government of the United Republic of Tanzania. http://reference.sabinet.co.za/webx/access/ journal_archive/00020117/33.pdf.

"The Price of Peace: Securing UN Financing for AU Peace Operations." 2020. Africa Report no. 286. *International Crisis Group.* www.crisisgroup.org/ africa/286-price-peace-securing-un-financing-au-peace-operations.

"The Principle of Subsidiarity: The Example of ECCAS in African Crises." 2016. Economic Community of Central African States/ Crisis Management Initiative. http://cmi.fi/wp-content/uploads/2017/03/ Principle_of_Subsidiarity_ECCAS_CMI_English.pdf.

"The Responsibility to Protect." 2001. International Commission on Intervention and State Sovereignty. http://responsibilitytoprotect.org/ ICISS%20Report.pdf.

Tieku, Thomas Kwasi. 2004. "Explaining the Clash and Accommodation of Major Actors in the Creation of the African Union." *African Affairs* 103 (411): 249–67.

2016. *Governing Africa: 3D Analysis of the African Union's Performance.* Routledge.

Tramontana, Enzamaria. 2010. "The Contribution of the Inter-American Human Rights Bodies to Evolving International Law on Indigenous Rights over Lands and Natural Resources." *International Journal on Minority and Group Rights* 17: 241–63.

Ulfstein, Geir. 2012. "Individual Complaints." In *UN Human Rights Treaty Bodies: Law and Legitimacy,* edited by Hellen Keller and Geir Ulfstein, 73–115. Cambridge University Press.

"UN Verification Mission in Colombia." n.d. United Nations. Accessed June 28, 2022. https://colombia.unmissions.org/en/mandate.

"Universal Declaration of Human Rights." 1948. United Nations. www.un.org/en/universal-declaration-human-rights/.

van Alebeek, Rosanne, and André Nollkaemper. 2012. "The Legal Status of Decisions by Human Rights Treaty Bodies in National Law." In *UN Human Rights Treaty Bodies: Law and Legitimacy,* edited by Helen Keller and Geir Ulfstein, 356–413. Cambridge University Press.

Velasquez Rodriquez v. Honduras. 1988. Inter-American Court of Human Rights.

Viljoen, Frans. 2019. "Impact in the African and Inter-American Human Rights Systems: A Perspective on the Possibilities and Challenges of Cross-Regional Comparison." In *The Inter-American Human Rights System,* edited by Par Engstrom, 303–26. Palgrave Macmillan.

von Staden, Andreas. 2016. "Subsidiarity in Regional Integration Regimes in Latin America and Africa." *Law and Contemporary Problems* 79 (2): 27–52.

Weiffen, Brigitte. 2012. "Persistence and Change in Regional Security Institutions: Does the OAS Still Have a Project?" *Contemporary Security Policy* 33 (2): 360–83. https://doi.org/10.1080/13523260.2012.693801.

Weiffen, Brigitte, Leslie Wehner, and Detlef Nolte. 2013. "Overlapping Regional Security Institutions in South America: The Case of OAS and UNASUR." *International Area Studies Review* 16 (4): 370–89.

"What Is the I/A Court H.R.?" n.d. Inter-American Court of Human Rights.

"What We Do." n.d. AHA Centre ASEAN. Accessed June 10, 2022. https://ahacentre.org/what-we-do/.

Wheeler, Nicholas J. 2000. *Saving Strangers: Humanitarian Intervention in International Society.* Oxford University Press.

Williams, Paul D. 2007. "From Non-Intervention to Non-Indifference: The Origins and Development of the African Union's Security Culture." *African Affairs* 106 (423): 253–79.

2011. "The African Union's Peace Operations: A Comparative Analysis." In *Regional Organizations in African Security,* edited by Fredrik Soderbaum and Rodrigo Tavares, 29–50. Routledge.

Wittke, Cindy. 2019. "The Minsk Agreements – More than 'Scraps of Paper'?" *East European Politics* 35 (3): 264–90.

Young, Oran. 1996. "Institutional Linkages in International Society: Polar Perspectives." *Global Governance* 2 (1): 1–23.

Zimmermann, Lisbeth, Nicole Deitelhoff, and Max Lesch. 2017. "Unlocking the Agency of the Governed: Contestation and Norm Dynamics." *Third World Thematics* 5 (2): 691–708.

Acknowledgments

The authors would like to acknowledge the generous support of Jon Pevehouse and Tanja Börzel in developing this Element. We would also like to thank Oumar Ba and an anonymous reviewer for their helpful comments during the review process.

This Element is the culmination of a years-long collaboration between the authors that has drawn on the support of the Peace and Conflict Resolution Evidence Platform (PeaceRep) at the University of Edinburgh Law School. We would like to thank the PeaceRep team for their feedback and support over the years as we developed our dataset of regional and global engagement in peace agreements and produced our findings.

This research is supported by the Peace and Conflict Resolution Evidence Platform (PeaceRep), funded by the UK Foreign, Commonwealth & Development Office (FCDO) for the benefit of developing countries. The information and views set out in this publication are those of the authors. Nothing herein constitutes the views of FCDO. Any use of this work should acknowledge the authors and the Peace and Conflict Resolution Evidence Platform.

Cambridge Elements ☰

International Relations

Series Editors

Jon C. W. Pevehouse
University of Wisconsin–Madison

Jon C. W. Pevehouse is the Vilas Distinguished Achievement Professor of Political Science at the University of Wisconsin–Madison. He has published numerous books and articles in IR in the fields of international political economy, international organizations, foreign policy analysis, and political methodology. He is a former editor of the leading IR field journal, International Organization.

Tanja A. Börzel
Freie Universität Berlin

Tanja A. Börzel is Professor of Political Science and holds the Chair for European Integration at the Otto-Suhr-Institute for Political Science, Freie Universität Berlin. She holds a PhD from the European University Institute, Florence, Italy. She is coordinator of the Research College "The Transformative Power of Europe," as well as the FP7-Collaborative Project "Maximizing the Enlargement Capacity of the European Union" and the H2020 Collaborative Project "The EU and Eastern Partnership Countries: An Inside-Out Analysis and Strategic Assessment." She directs the Jean Monnet Center of Excellence "Europe and Its Citizens."

Edward D. Mansfield
University of Pennsylvania

Edward D. Mansfield is the Hum Rosen Professor of Political Science, University of Pennsylvania. He has published well over 100 books and articles in the area of international political economy, international security, and international organizations. He is Director of the Christopher H. Browne Center for International Politics at the University of Pennsylvania and former program co-chair of the American Political Science Association.

Editorial Team

About the series

The Cambridge Elements Series in International Relations publishes original research on key topics in the field. The series includes manuscripts addressing international security, international political economy, international organizations, and international relations.

Cambridge Elements ≡

International Relations

Elements in the Series

Weak States at Global Climate Negotiations
Federica Genovese

Social Media and International Relations
Sarah Kreps

Across Type, Time and Space: American Grand Strategy in Comparative Perspective
Peter Dombrowski and Simon Reich

Moral Psychology, Neuroscience, and International Norms
Richard Price and Kathryn Sikkink

Contestations of the Liberal International Order
Fredrik Söderbaum, Kilian Spandler, Agnese Pacciardi

Domestic Interests, Democracy, and Foreign Policy Change
Brett Ashley Leeds, Michaela Mattes

Token Forces: How Tiny Troop Deployments Became Ubiquitous in UN Peacekeeping
Katharina P. Coleman, Xiaojun Li

The Dual Nature of Multilateral Development Banks
Laura Francesca Peitz

Peace in Digital International Relations
Oliver P. Richmond, Gëzim Visoka, Ioannis Tellidis

Regionalized Governance in the Global South
Brooke Coe, Kathryn Nash

A full series listing is available at: www.cambridge.org/EIR

Printed in the United States
by Baker & Taylor Publisher Services